Dear Dad
Happy Birthday
lots of love
IAN
+
Christy

FAMOUS
FORD WOODIES

FAMOUS
FORD WOODIES

BY LORIN SORENSEN

Above: *An American snapshot. Mom and the kids with the family's brand-new 1950 Ford Station Wagon.*

Left: *The Cook family from Michigan on a vacation with the second Ford woodie made – C.W. Avery's 1928 Model A.*

SILVERADO PUBLISHING COMPANY, ST. HELENA, CALIFORNIA
and Ten Speed Press, Berkeley / Toronto

Published by Silverado Publishing Company
P.O. Box 393
St. Helena, California 94574

Available from Ten Speed Press
P.O. Box 7123
Berkeley, California, 94707
www.tenspeed.com

Distributed in Australia by Simon & Schuster Australia, in Canada by Ten Speed Press Canada, in New Zealand by Southern Publishers Group, in South Africa by Real Books, and in the United Kingdom and Europe by Airlift Book Company.

Typesetting by Ellen Peters

Art and photo production by David Fetherston

Edited by Cliff and Cara Swartz

ISBN NO. 1-58008-548-2
Printed in China

First printing, 2003
1 2 3 4 5 6 7 8 9 10 – 08 07 06 05 04 03

ACKNOWLEDGMENTS

A word about my spelling of "woodie" – in the singular – on these pages. That's the way it's intentionally spelled by the National Woodie Club.

This book probably took root one April day in 1964 when I caught a flash of wood going the other way on a curve outside my hometown of Santa Rosa, California. It was the late Mr. G.L. Thunberg in his immaculate maroon '40 Ford Deluxe station wagon. I bought it the next day. It turned out to be body number 11725 —according to the records, the last '40 Ford wagon produced! It's been a member of our family since.

A special thanks to those who said I should write this book. It wasn't my idea. Doug Clem, Nick Alexander, Dan Krehbiel, Jim Edison, 2003 National Woodie Club President Craig Johnson, and others — you convinced me!

Thanks Dennis Carpenter and Bob Jones, for sharing your Ford literature collections. Thanks again Dan Brooks for your assistance with the Ford photo research. And to Tim Johnstone, editor of *Wagon Wheels*, for your great help with the Model As, and Tim Conner whose knowledge of the '49-51s has been an education. And, as always, thanks to Sandy Notarriani, of Ford-Canada, and to the staffs of Ford and the Henry Ford Museum Research Center.

By chance, auto historian Henry Dominguez interviewed legendary Ford chief stylist Bob Gregorie for me just three weeks before he died at 94. It was his last ever interview! Thanks, Henry. Also, many thanks to Ross Cousins and Tucker Madawick for your awesome first-hand stories about working for Gregorie.

Brad Smith sent me a note about a collection of original woodie photos bought some years ago from a used book store. It was obviously that of Dr. Tom Garrett, the late Ford *Sportsman* authority. Some of the prints I gave to Tom back in time. Thanks Brad, for sharing this bonanza with us as noted on these pages.

C.W. Avery's grandson, Avery Greene, is a story by himself (as noted on page 16). Thanks again Avery. I guess it was meant to be. Thanks Tim Krehbiel and Alex De Ulloa. Your wealth of Ford woodie knowledge is terrific!

Many thanks to my longtime assistant Ellen Peters, and to David Fetherston (you know him, he wrote the book, *American Woodys*) for their technical skills. A big thanks also to Ralph Hubbard for his good advice, and to Ed Clarke, Glen Hague, Pat McGarity, Al Finseth, Cliff Helling, Barrett McGregor, Mike Welch, Don Chew, Al Hesselbart, Budd Steinhilber, Ray Beniquez, Ted Carpenter, Jerry Veley, "Woody Bob" Johnson, Ron Love, Kent Jaquith, and to everyone who has helped me on this project. *LORIN SORENSEN* ◆

CONTENTS

Golden wood. Long golden summers. Handy for whatever lay around the bend, a handsome '39 Ford Deluxe Station Wagon makes a stop at a roadside fruit stand near Palm Springs, Calif.

Right: Within a decade the Ford station wagon went from utility vehicle to the darling of high-society. A sporty new '40 Deluxe model meets the plane at Ford Airport in Dearborn, Michigan.

Photo courtesy of Ford Motor Company

The perfect weekend getaway before motels was a sporty new '49 Mercury Station Wagon with a cozy Vagabond trailer. Ford created the woodcrafted station wagon market and these unique 1929 to 1951 "woodies" are among the most recognized and desirable of American cars ever produced.

The top Ford men in 1919, looking for Michigan timberland

"No one can follow these extra-automotive activities without recognizing the daring and flexibility of a mind. Here Ford is fully the industrial and social pioneer." NEVINS & HILL, FORD; EXPANSION AND CHALLENGE

Henry Ford (hatless) and his son Edsel (arms folded) are pictured in 1919 with their key men outside the Yeazel Hotel in Frankfort, Michigan. From the left are production men Peter E. Martin and Charles E. Sorensen, business manager Frank L. Klingensmith, and factory construction boss William S. Knudsen. At the right in top coat is development engineer Clarence W. Avery. The group was in Frankfort looking for property to locate a much-needed Model T woodworks. Henry Ford would find what he was looking for further west at Iron Mountain where he put Avery in charge.

INTRODUCTION

Ford, Iron Mountain

This book illustrates the story of those beautifully-crafted Ford "woodie" station wagons built between the fall of 1928, and the last one that, by chance, came off the line on my 16th birthday December 5, 1951. Today, they are all rightly considered true American classics. Each one was hand made and uniquely different from any other. But the one thing common to them all was the hardwood used to make their famous maple and birch bodies. It all came from a now legendary place called Iron Mountain.

The tale has its beginning here in the northern forests of Michigan's Upper Peninsula in the spring of 1920 when Henry Ford took an option on some land he thought had great potential. That summer, he took his top men, including his son Edsel and chief development engineer Clarence W. Avery, up Lake Michigan in his steam yacht *Sialia* to look over its possibilities.

Years later in a speech before a gathering of early Ford employees, Avery would recall that trip. Especially the lighter side of the usually reserved Mr. Ford. "Frank Klingensmith," said Avery, "who was Ford Treasurer at that time, had just acquired a new watch, of which he was very proud. It was the best that money could buy. As we stood on ship's deck, the watch was being displayed. Mr. Ford said, 'Let's see that watch.' He turned it over and over in his hand, looking at it very carefully, and finally said, 'Nothing but a cheap imitation — no good at all!' With that he hurled it on the deck of the ship, and it broke into a thousand pieces.

"Frank said, 'Oh, Mr. Ford! My watch'," and his face revealed almost every emotion known to man. He got down on the deck and picked up as many pieces as he could find, and carefully wrapped them in a piece of paper, and put them in his pocket. From time to time, he confided his feelings to the rest of us. 'Why do you suppose he did it?' 'Do you suppose Mr. Ford will buy me a new watch?' — and many other questions.

"Several days later, his watch turned up, good as ever, on his breakfast plate. A cheap imitation had been deftly substituted for the real watch."

Down to business, the Ford men took a look at the Iron Mountain property. It was a huge tract of some 313,000 acres of virgin forest. Henry Ford had already explored the site. He calculated that its dense hardwood stands of maple, birch, basswood and hemlock might furnish him with years of wood for such parts as floorboards, roof ribs, body framing and shipping crates essential for making his millions of Model Ts.

It was typical of Ford to think on a grand scale. What he envisioned was a factory up here to mass-produce wood parts for his cars, like he made steel parts in Detroit. Key to his plan was Avery, who had a genius for mass-production.

The river would provide free hydroelectric power. Nearby docks gave cheap access to shipping. The town of Iron Mountain would supply the work force.

Local realtor E.G. Kingsford, a cousin of Ford's by marriage arranged the sale. He showed him an additional tract that could be purchased. It was a good place to build a sawmill Ford needed for a reliable source of wood. The famed industrialist ordered the deal done and returned home with his group. That September, he incorporated the Michigan Iron, Land, and Lumber Company, putting Clarence W. Avery in charge.

By 1923, the Iron Mountain complex was a beehive of activity with its own logging crews and 7,000 employees working around the clock to produce Ford wood. The heart of the system was a huge lumber mill with power carriages running whole logs through giant band saws to make green slabs which would go first to the big dry kilns, then to the planers, and then to the fabricating shops to be made into finished Model T parts.

Nothing was wasted. All the scrap wood was made into the world's first commercial charcoal briquets, or sent on to the plant's big distilleries to be made into useful by-products like wood alcohol, or the ethyl acetate used for making artificial leather for Ford tops and upholstery. Ford ran the town, the rail lines going in and out, and what amounted to — the entire Iron Mountain area economy.

When the time came, it was the perfect place to supply the hardwood and materials needed to build high-quality Ford station wagon bodies. *LORIN SORENSEN*

"A number of years ago, I was delegated the job of developing the Ford timber project in Northern Michigan. When the sawmill was completed and in production, Mr. Ford was inspecting the results. 'Well,' he said, with that familiar twinkle in his eye, 'you have done a good job so far, but there is one thing more. You are cutting rectangular boards out of round logs, and that is very wasteful. You must now learn how to grow square trees.'" C.W. AVERY, IN SPEECH AT DINNER FOR FORD MOTOR COMPANY 35-YEAR EMPLOYEES AT THE DEARBORN INN, DECEMBER 19, 1944. Courtesy of the Avery Greene family archives

(Note: Avery did grow the square trees as an experiment that didn't work very well. He later presented a polished cross section of one as a joke to Henry Ford.)

Henry Ford at 62 in 1925

THE WAGONWORKS

Source of all the hardwood for Ford station wagons, the Iron Mountain plant began supplying lumber for Model Ts in 1921. The company soon built an airfield and new homes in the town of Iron Mountain (pictured, 1951 population 14,560) to attract employees. By the time this photo was taken in 1946 the plant had grown into a huge operation with its own hydroelectric plant, rail line, sawmills, dry kilns, and chemical distillery. About 2,000 workers were turning out handcrafted station wagon bodies. In its best times, Iron Mountain also furnished wood for other car makers. At various times it also produced wood patterns for making airplanes and ships, furnished wood for railroad cars, and from its scrap wood was the largest producer of charcoal briquets in the world.

The plant, located on the Menominee River border between Michigan and Wisconsin, closed at the end of station wagon production in 1951.

Photo courtesy of Ford Motor Company

The Ford Iron Mountain plant in 1946. At the height of production it was the largest woodworking complex in the world.

1930 Model A Ford Station Wagon

1928

BODY BY MURRAY

1939

Clarence Willard Avery, 1882–1949

"One day in the '70s while on a family outing with my pride and joy original '40 Ford Deluxe wagon near our home in the Napa Valley, we stopped at a park for lunch. A young fellow about my age came over and said, 'Nice car.' Then, 'Ever hear of Clarence Avery?' I said, Sure. He invented the Ford moving assembly line. 'Well,' came the reply, 'He was my grandfather.' It was Avery Greene, just moved from Michigan, a new auto dealer in nearby Vallejo, a new friend, and when it came time to write this book, the primary source of the remarkable C.W. Avery story as set down on these pages." LORIN SORENSEN, author

C.W. AVERY
production genius

Iron Mountain furnished the hardwood for the wood-bodied Ford station wagons. The man who had the biggest hand in building them from beginning to end was the inventive C.W. Avery of Murray Corporation of America.

Avery was one of the most important men in the early development of Ford Motor Company. In fact, he is recognized as one of the most important men in all automobile history – being inducted into the Automotive Hall of Fame as designer of "the first moving assembly line for mass production of automobiles."

A man of great ability, Avery was born February 15, 1882, in Dansville, Michigan. He later attended the University of Michigan and, in 1907, became director of manual training at Detroit University School. It was here in 1908 that he met fourteen-year-old Edsel Ford who had enrolled in one of his classes to prepare himself to work in his father's company. Edsel soon became so impressed with his teacher's clever mechanics that in 1912 he got the 30-year-old Avery a job at Ford Motor Company as assistant to production boss Charles Sorensen.

As Ford R. Bryan notes in his excellent book, *Henry's Lieutenants*, "Within a year, Avery, Sorensen, and others were involved in establishing the moving final assembly line for automobiles."

Avery was considered the guiding light in this historic endeavor. By 1913, Highland Park was building six times as many Model Ts per man-hour as the old stationary line. In developing the moving assembly line, Avery also perfected the art of time study, and designed speedy sub-assembly operations to feed the final line.

By now he was the company's chief development engineer, and one of Henry Ford's top five men. Soon he became Ford's glass expert, designing huge new plants to make the gigantic amount of plate glass needed for Model T windshields and windows. In doing so, he invented an ingenious continuous line process that revolutionized the industry.

In 1920, Avery was put in charge of developing Ford's big Northern Michigan Iron, Land, and Lumber Company at Iron Mountain. Like the mass-production of glass, this enormous wood operation would produce floorboards and body parts for the millions of Ford cars and trucks.

The quick-minded Avery wore a number of hats at Ford, besides the one handed him at Iron Mountain.

When Henry Ford bought Lincoln Motor Car Company from the Leland family in 1922, he gave it to his son Edsel to run. Edsel called on his good friend Avery to help bring some class to the stodgy line of cars. Avery was then instrumental in lining up custom body producers like Willoughby and Dietrich to provide the great coachwork that would become the hallmark of Edsel's elegant Lincolns.

But central as he was to so much of Ford's success, Avery was not immune to some of the infighting among Henry Ford's chief lieutenants. In 1927, after one such incident he resigned despite Edsel's best efforts to patch over the dispute.

According to Ford historian David L. Lewis, Avery was one of the few important figures of Henry Ford's day who left the company with the warm friendship and admiration of "the old man."

Avery soon took a top position with the Murray Corporation, a well-known Detroit company founded by J.W. Murray, "the dean of stamping manufacturers." Murray was a major supplier of stampings for the auto industry. Its Murray Body division built finished custom bodies for Ford as well as for Packard, Reo, Marmon, and Hudson.

It is probable that Avery's Lincoln relationship with Murray's Dietrich Body subsidiary drew him to Murray. It is even more likely that Murray, which had just emerged from receivership with a band of new investors, hoped C.W. Avery would be the man to reenergize the company with his abilities and connections.

Avery began at Murray as chief engineer and manufacturing manager and within one year was named president and chairman of the board of the company that would soon be building the historic first Ford station wagons.◆

Edsel Ford 1893–1943

"At the end of the school year, in June, 1912, (Edsel Ford) and I entered Ford Motor Company almost the same day, as students of the automotive industry. A few years later, he became president, and our 'young boss' as we so fondly called him. In later years, I knew him as a customer for Murray products, and as an associate in several civic activities. He was always modest, capable, sincere and considerate and ever a loyal friend. The passing of no other (Edsel died May 26, 1943) outside my own family, could affect me so much." C.W. AVERY, IN SPEECH AT DINNER FOR FORD MOTOR COMPANY 35-YEAR EMPLOYEES AT THE DEARBORN INN, DECEMBER 19, 1944 Courtesy of the Avery Greene family archives

EDSEL, AVERY, AND THE WOODIE

The name of the man whose idea it was to create a Ford station wagon in 1928 was never written down. It didn't need to be. The fact that Edsel Ford kept the first one for himself and gave the second one to his longtime friend C.W. Avery, president and chairman of the board of Murray Corporation of America, pretty well tells the story.

It isn't hard to understand why Edsel Ford wanted a rustic wood-bodied station wagon added to the Ford line. It simply fit his own personal lifestyle. As president of Ford Motor Company, and the son of one of the world's wealthiest men, Edsel lived the sporting life of high-society. He had a rambling estate on Lake St. Clair Shores in Detroit with a garage full of custom Lincolns, Packards, and Cadillacs; he was an avid yachtsman, with several sloops; his boat house was full of fast mahogany speedboats that he raced on weekends; and he spent boating, tennis and golfing getaways at some of the best resorts, or at his family's winter home on Hobe Sound in Florida, or their new summer home at Seal Harbor, Maine.

While living something of a Great Gatsby lifestyle, Edsel was at the same time conservative-thinking and hardworking. A natural-born automobile stylist, he directed all the great Ford designs from the company's first Lincolns and Model As to those unfinished when he died suddenly at age 49 in 1943.

Once Edsel decided to produce a new Ford-type, he usually made the decision after consulting with his close circle of advisers, production men Charles Sorensen and P.E. Martin, and body engineer Joe Galamb. They would then confer with the sales department.

In the case of a new wood-bodied utility, Edsel already had the numbers. For some time, the company had been tracking sales of custom body firms, notably Martin-Parry,

All photos in this chapter courtesy of the Henry Ford Museum Research Center, except where noted.

and Cantrell. They were doing considerable business selling custom "depot hack" bodies for the Model T chassis — and were now promoting similar bodies for the new Model A.

The depot hack had become a well-recognized veteran of the American motoring scene, often spotted on the East Coast meeting trains in a time when travelers had large steamer trunks that wouldn't fit in the back of regular cars. As taxis they did a good business delivering passengers to hotels and resorts.

The first production depot hack made by an American auto producer was the 1923 Star "Station Wagon," with a body by Mengel of Louisville, Kentucky. Poorly marketed, it soon faded away along with its nameplate.

With the influence of the depot hacks, it's easy to see why Edsel Ford decided to add one of these utility types to the Model A line, giving it a more refined station wagon designation. He asked his friend C.W. Avery, who built automobile bodies and knew all about wood from his years at Iron Mountain, to develop it.

Edsel also had a personal reason for wanting something like a station wagon.

Just completed in craggy granite-faced craftsman-style was "Skylands," his magnificent new twenty-one-room summer home and estate at Seal Harbor, Maine.

A smartly turned out wagon, with handcrafted, "Greene & Greene"-style wood panelling, might be just the thing for the caretaker to meet the train when they made their trips in *"Fairlane,"* the family's parlor car.

Avery was a sporting man himself and had his own country estate. He knew just what Edsel wanted. He also knew that any wagon body construction had to begin, not with the wood — but with the special sheet metal stampings needed: namely the cowl and floorpan. And this is where his company excelled.

Murray Stamping could produce nearly anything in sheet metal that could be drawn. With that in-house ability, Murray Body Division could build just about any car that could be dreamed. The Company had its own design department. But these were busy times, so outside consulting engineer T. Hardy Hays actually drew the first scale drawings of the proposed 1929 Ford Station Wagon.

His first effort was something of a baggage wagon, with no center side doors or rear seats. Between Ford and Murray body engineers this would evolve into drawings for a passenger-and-utility type station wagon design that had more sporting dash.

MENGEL BODY

Surprisingly, Ford's Iron Mountain plant did not furnish the finished wood parts for Murray to build the Model A station wagon bodies. Rather, Iron Mountain shipped kiln-dried hardwood planks to Mengel Body in Louisville, Kentucky. That company finished the wood parts and sub-assembly panels, then sent them to Murray in Detroit to combine with its metal stampings for the body-build and finish.

Edsel had good reasons for giving the job to Mengel. He wanted a top-quality automobile wood finisher with proven craftsmanship to make the parts for his Model A station wagon bodies. Iron Mountain at the time did not have that capability.

Mengel was one of the premier custom body builders in the country, turning out work for such nameplates as Chrysler, Franklin, and Packard. Mengel also had a good relationship with Ford, building specialty Model T bodies for Ford's Louisville branch and producing a school bus for the new Model AA line. In addition, as for the new Ford work, Mengel had good experience producing the wood bodies for the first Star station wagons.

So, in the fall of 1928, Murray completed the first prototype Model A Station Wagon. It was destined for Edsel's summer home in Maine. Soon after, the second prototype was built. This one Edsel gave to C.W. Avery to keep and road test. Avery's daughter, Annabelle Baxley, who was 7-years-old at the time, remembers it well. Down through the years, her family always referred to it as "the prototype".

"It was a wood-bodied station wagon developed by Murray for Ford", she says. "Dad drove it to get the bugs out before they went into production and I remember when we took a trip from Detroit to Colorado, and up Pike's Peak. Later, he sold it to Uncle Bill Cook who used it on camping trips."

In January, 1929, the first Ford station wagons were officially introduced. It was the beginning of one of the most memorable series of automobiles in American history.◆

Mengel Body of Louisville, Kentucky, produced the woodwork for the 1928-33 Ford station wagon bodies.

Top right: Inspiration for the first Ford station wagons were the popular depot hacks usually seen meeting the train. This Suburban model body by Huntington, N.Y. maker J.T. Cantrell & Co., is pictured on a 1923 Model T chassis.

Right: A Tacoma, Washington, grocer with his family and depot hack on a weekend outing in 1921. This was the kind of all-round work and pleasure use Edsel Ford envisioned for his Model A station wagon.

Edsel Ford wanted a wood-bodied "station wagon" like the old Model T depot hack, with more sporting dash.

American families had already discovered the versatility of the Model T depot hack.

FORD "WOODIE" NUMBER ONE – The first prototype Ford station wagon, a brilliant work of refined simplicity and understatement by Edsel Ford and C.W. Avery, went to Edsel's Skylands summer home.

HISTORIC FORD

A high-quality varnished maple body with a sporty roof line, and room for eight – all on the perky new 4-cylinder Model A chassis! Edsel Ford was so sure resorts and sporting families would go for his all-new wood-panelled "station wagon" that he ordered one for himself.

His milestone first woodie is pictured ready to leave Dearborn for Seal Harbor, Maine, where it would be used at Skylands, his new 21-room summer home and estate. (At this writing Skylands is owned by lifestyle maven Martha Stewart.)

FORD "WOODIE" NUMBER TWO — C.W. Avery's well-used original test prototype on a camping trip with his brother-in-law's family in 1936.

Edsel gave the second wagon built to his friend C.W. Avery of Murray Corp. to test drive and develop. A few years later he sold it to his brother-in-law Bill Cook (pictured with his son Bruce), right, a Detroit oral surgeon. Note that both prototype wagons have light-colored wheels and other interesting early features.

"It was a wood-bodied station wagon developed by Murray for Ford . . . Dad drove it to get the bugs out before they went into production . . ." ANNABELLE BAXLEY, C.W. AVERY'S DAUGHTER

1929 Model A Ford exhibit at Salt Lake City

Beyond a snazzy new *Sport Coupe* on display with other Fords at the Salt Lake City assembly plant in October, 1929, is a rare sighting of a Model A *Station Wagon*. While admirable, the "commercial" maple and birch wagons were slow to catch on. They were usually assigned to the back row of such events with the trucks until 1938 when they earned a rightful place up front with the passenger line.

Photo courtesy of the Salt Lake City Historical Society

FORD MODEL A STATION WAGON Model 150-A
1929-30 production – 6,529

$650 Detroit

Body by Murray

NEW FORD STATION WAGON

Making their public debut in early 1929, the first Ford station wagons were initially promoted for use of "country clubs and estates." And they looked the part with jaunty lines, sporty interiors, and richly varnished Craftsman-style *maple*, *birch* and *basswood* bodies. They set a standard that would last for the next two decades.

The new Ford *Station Wagon* is a most valuable addition to country clubs and estates because of its high utility value. Added to this is good appearance. It has comfortable seating for eight, with ample space for luggage on the lowered tailgate, should it be required. Rear seats are removed to convert the car into a haulage unit, providing a large loading space. The body combines rugged attractiveness with rugged construction. A wide seat in the driver's compartment will seat three passengers. Wide doors are hung on piano hinges. FORD NEWS, JANUARY 2, 1929

1929 Model A Station Wagon

1929-31 FORD STATION WAGON
Specifications in general

CHASSIS & EQUIPMENT – 103 1/2" wheel-base. 40 h.p. 4-cylinder engine. Standard equipment includes spare tire carried in the left fender well, side curtains, tools, sideview mirror, automatic windshield wiper, and gas gauge.

BODY

Natural hard *Maple* framing. *Birch* ply-wood panels. *Basswood* roof slats. Top material is *Black* coarse long-short grain artificial leather.

INTERIOR

150-A seats are upholstered in *Blue-Grey Colonial-grain* artificial leather and 150-B seats in dark two-tone cross *Cobra-grain* artificial leather. Tan rubber inter-lined side curtain material to harmonize with the body finish. Heavy celluloid windows. *Black* rubber floor mats in compartments.

COLORS (hood and cowl)

MANILA BROWN
BLACK fenders

Source:
1929-31 Ford factory sale letters
1929-31 Ford sales literature
1929-31 *FORD NEWS*
Tim Johnstone, Editor, *WAGON WHEELS*
Model A Ford Club of America,
Judging Standards & Restoration Guidelines

Murray's execution of the 1929 Ford station wagon bodies showed skillful design and quality woodcraft. The natural-grain birch panelling was set off in rich counterpoint to the maple framing, while the special hardware and bolt patterns provided strength as well as art. A pair of center seats in these pioneering models were split so passengers could move to the back. Storage for the side curtains was located under the rear floor. Ford manufactured its own artificial leather for the seats and roof fabric.

MURRAY AND BAKER-RAULANG
1930-32

"Baker-Raulang Co., of Cleveland, Ohio, has been awarded a contract by the Ford Motor Co. for the building of station wagon bodies in quantities ranging from 25 to 100 per day, depending on demand." AUTOBODY, May, 1930

A new Model A "150-B" body was planned for 1930-31. Murray Corp. was given the job to produce the design, draftings and drawings. Production was scheduled to begin in March, 1930.

Ford specified that the wood for these units was to be "hard or soft maple, free from checks or warps. No knot hearts permitted. Moisture content not to exceed 12%."

After getting the job to build the bodies at $203.95 each, Murray found that it was so overwhelmed with other work that production start-up on the station wagon bodies was being delayed.

Other work from Ford was the cause of Murray's problem. It had just won big contracts to begin supplying 1930 bodies for the new Victoria sedan model, all the large and small Model A and AA panel deliveries, and several other new commercial types.

So, Murray president, C.W. Avery — his production capacity stretched — gave up a good share of the new Model A station wagon job to a respected competitor — Baker-Raulang Company, of Cleveland, Ohio. Still, production would not start until the first of June.

At that time, three companies besides Ford produced most of the bodies for the hot-selling Model A line. Briggs Body Company of Detroit was the biggest, making mostly sedans, Murray made the specialty types, and Budd Company of Philadelphia turned out the commercials.

BAKER-RAULANG COMPANY

When Baker-Raulang got the order from Ford to build a major share of the new-style 1930 Ford station wagon bodies, it was long established as a major custom body builder for the auto industry. Their clients included prestigious names such as Dusenberg, Peerless, and Reo. They were also producing the nation's most luxurious line of long-distance bus bodies, with top-quality hardwood panelling, soft leather seats, and the patented overhead "Luggage Loft."

It was their top-quality bus work that made them most suitable to build the new Ford wagons. It was also helpful that Henry Ford and the firm's principal owner were old friends.

Ford and Walter C. Baker were cut from the same cloth. They were both automobile visionaries: Baker, of Cleveland, betting that the electric car was the answer — Ford, of Detroit, betting on the gasoline-powered machine.

Both men owed their early success to racing. At Grosse Pointe, Michigan, in 1901, Henry Ford beat Alexander Winton, the world speed record holder for the automobile over a timed distance. With his $1,000 winnings, Ford was able to launch the Ford Motor Company.

Walter Baker was already in the automobile business. Since 1899 he had been manufacturing and selling the Baker Electric. One of his first customers was Thomas Edison. In 1902, with Henry Ford an interested assistant,

All photos in this chapter courtesy of the Henry Ford Museum Research Center, except where noted.

1930 Model A Ford Station Wagon

Baker astounded the world when at Ormond Beach, Florida, his special electric "Torpedo" racecar set the world speed record for an automobile at 104 mph!

Auto fans were suddenly mad about electrics. But it was a short-lived mania, and Henry Ford, with his low-priced gasoline-powered Model T, had bet on the winner.

There's more to the Ford-Baker connection. Henry Ford owed much of his Model T's astounding success to his advertising of the discovery and use of the virtually unbreakable "vanadium" steel alloy used in the running gear. The fact is, Walter Baker and his shops made the vanadium steel alloy discovery while experimenting with lightweight steel for their battery-powered cars. They then sold Henry Ford an order of 10,000 vanadium front axle forgings for his 1909 Model T. By the time they were installed, Henry Ford was running his own vanadium for Model T production and his company would go down in auto history as the originator of the famous "impossible-to-twist-or-break" steel.

In 1915, the Baker Motor Vehicle Company merged with its main U.S. competitor, the long-established Rauch and Lang Carriage Company, also of Cleveland, which produced the Rauch and Lang electric car.

The merger would create the Baker-Raulang Company, which soon began producing the sensational new gasoline-powered "Car of a Thousand Speeds" Owens Magnetic. Featuring a novel electric transmission, it was considered America's first no-shift automobile.

During World War I Baker-Raulang began producing electric industrial trucks used in ship building, and, in 1919, formed two divisions: one for the industrial truck production, and the other for the production of custom automobile bodies.

Following World War II their automobile body operations were discontinued, and they expanded industrial truck production. By 1952 the Baker-Raulang Company had transformed to become the Towmotor Company, one of the largest manufacturers of electric forklifts.

There is a footnote to the Baker-Raulang/Ford connection. George Walker, Ford's flamboyant styling consultant and chief stylist from 1948 to 1959, began his career in automotive design working for Walter Baker. After Baker, he worked for General Motors, Graham-Paige, and then Ford.

In 1930, when Baker's company made the deal with C.W. Avery to build some of the new-styled Model A station wagon bodies, there were evidently some conditions attached. One of which allowed Baker-Raulang to build the wood bodies — less the stamped metal cowls that Murray alone produced. These would be added later at the Ford assembly plants. It was a clever move to keep control of the Ford station wagon job. When things returned to normal at Murray, Ford would transfer all the station wagon work back to them. To prove their readiness, Murray built some of the bodies in Detroit complete in every respect, including the cowls.

(This created one of those Ford production oddities; the usual sequential numbering of wagon bodies for quality control was all but abandoned on the Model 150-B job.)

Ford stopped Model A production in mid-1931 to make the changeover to Henry Ford's breakthrough low-priced V-8 engine. However, the V-8 development took so long, it was March, 1932, before the new models came off the line.

Meanwhile, production of commercial cars and Model AA trucks was continued. Murray Corporation of America was supplying many of the bodies for these models, as well as bodies for other auto makers.

At the same time they were tooling up for the new 1932 Fords. All this activity again brought Murray's capacity to the limit. Once more, they looked to Baker-Raulang for help with the new station wagon job. As before, it was agreed that the bodies were to be built without the front cowls. Murray would produce and ship the cowls directly to the Ford assembly plants for installation. (This time Baker-Raulang, which evidently used another system of quality control, made no attempt to number the bodies.)

From the record, the first 1932 Ford station wagon body completed with chassis came off the line at the Ford Chester, Pennsylvania, assembly plant in May 1932. ◆

Walter C. Baker in his electric "Torpedo" racer in 1902 after setting the world speed record of 104 m.p.h.!

A 1931 Ford commercial car and truck exhibit at Louisville, Kentucky.

Commercial models at a public open house held at Ford's Louisville, Kentucky, assembly plant include among the trucks one of the top-quality new 1931 Model A station wagons. These units were little different from the 1930, except for restyled grille shell (near right) and other slight changes associated with the 1931 line.

A 1930 Model A Station Wagon stands on the floor of Henry Ford's grand Highland Park showroom in Detroit. It was a typical scene from any given day during the 1930s, with all the gleaming passenger cars and truck models proudly displayed.

1930 FORD MODEL A STATION WAGON Model 150-B
1930 production – 2,229
1931 production – 3,018

$650 Detroit

Body by Baker-Raulang, or Murray

A close-up of the new *"150-B"* 1930 Model A *Station Wagon* pictured opposite reveals a crisply-executed body and side curtains, with *Manila Brown* hood and cowl coordinated with the varnished wood body. Spacers under the tires protect Henry Ford's beloved polished floors. The newly styled "150-B" body with rounder sloping roof line was introduced in mid-1930 and was built through the end of 1931. It was a nicely-crafted combination of Murray plans and stampings, Ford, Iron Mountain hardwood, Mengel Body woodwork, and Baker-Raulang or Murray assembly and trim. Ford purchasing records show that Murray charged Ford $205 for each finished 150-B body, as pictured.

One of the unique '31 Ford Special Deliveries was featured in a Los Angeles dealer promotion.

-1932-

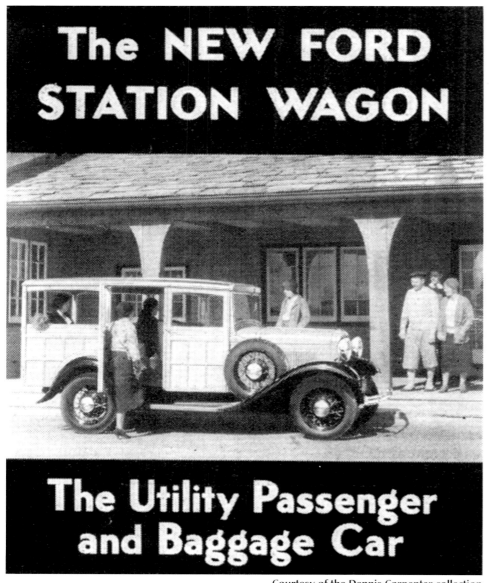

The NEW FORD STATION WAGON

The Utility Passenger and Baggage Car

Courtesy of the Dennis Carpenter collection

By 1932, the sporting Ford *Station Wagon* was all the rage with the country club set. This was the year Henry Ford introduced his famous "flathead Ford V-8" and the handsome wagon, while initially offered only as the 4-cylinder "Model B," was given extra status a month later when it was also made available with the V-8. The plain commercial car front-end styling was standard and without lifting the hood the eight cylinder models could be identified by the "V-8" emblem on the headlight bar and hubcaps.

1932 "MODEL B"

The new Ford *Station Wagon* stands unique in the field. "Air Cushion" seats throughout and instant protection afforded by the new channel-slide side curtains make this semi-enclosed, general utility car outstanding. Curtains rest in brass channels in roof when not in use and may be pulled down instantly into close-fitting window and door channels. *1932 FORD COMMERCIAL CARS.*

***1932 FORD STATION WAGON** Model B-150*
Production – 1,032 with 4-cylinder engine, and 351 with V-8

$600 Detroit

Body by Baker-Raulang

No Hollywood film star was ever a bigger Ford fan than character actor Wallace Beery, who bought new ones nearly every year. He is pictured getting ready for a trip with his latest — a handy '32 *Station Wagon* — after finishing "*Grand Hotel,*" his 55th movie. Beery's wagon has been changed to softer-riding 14-inch super balloon tires and wheels. With passenger car front features and a tan top, this may be one of the rare "deluxe" V-8 models reported built that year.

Below: Like the Model As, the '32 Ford station wagons took woodwork design cues from the interior lattice panelling of the popular Craftsman-style home.

Wallace Beery loads his custom-equipped '32 wagon.

The well-executed '32 Ford wagon was panelled like a Green & Green Craftsman bungalow.

1932 FORD STATION WAGON
Specifications in general

CHASSIS & EQUIPMENT – 106-inch wheelbase. 50 h.p. 4-cylinder engine. Standard equipment includes 5:50x18 4-ply tires, right well fender with spare cover and lock, and side-mirror. (In June, 1932, the 65-h.p V-8 engine was made available as an option at an extra $50.)

BODY

Frame is *Maple.* Panels are *Birch* plywood. *Basswood* roof slats. Top fabric color is B-153310 *Black* artificial leather.

INTERIOR

Seats are two-tone *Black Brown Fine Colonial Grain* artificial leather. Side curtains are tan fabric. *Tan* rubber floor mats.

COLORS (Hood and cowl)

MANILA BROWN (early)
WINTER LEAF BROWN (mid-year)
EMPEROR BROWN (late)
BLACK fenders

SOURCE:
1932 Ford Body Parts List
1932 Ford factory sales letters
Dealer sales literature

Built by the shops of Baker-Raulang Company, of Cleveland, the '32 Ford *Station Wagon* body had all the same fine hardwood craftsmanship of the Murray company which couldn't handle the production this model year. The tail gate hinged down with leather-covered chains to make a platform for luggage. The side curtains were now stored in the ceiling on brass slide channels. The tools stored in a box under the rear floor.

The open windows of a well-worn '34 Ford station wagon make it handy for a Connecticut dairy driver to make home deliveries in 1938.

1933-34

MURRAY AND IRON MOUNTAIN
1933-39

From the beginning, Murray Corporation of America, under C.W. Avery, handled just about every aspect of Ford station wagon body production, from engineering, to developing the pilot models, to furnishing the sheet metal stampings.

Their chief body designer was Amos Northrup, who supervised the Murray work on all the Ford station wagon bodies from the start. He was also responsible for the designs of the Ford A and B-400 convertible sedans, and the new 1933-34 wagon series. Besides Fords, he also designed bodies for Lincoln and for other Murray clients such as Packard. Considered one of the best custom body designers in Detroit, his life was cut short one day in 1934 when he slipped on an icy sidewalk, struck his head, and died.

These were gloomy times. Like the rest of the auto industry, work at Murray had reached Depression lows. Among the bright spots, however, Ford placed an initial order for 500 of the redesigned 1933 station wagon bodies, with more to come on an as-needed-basis. The new Fords were behind schedule, so delivery was set for March.

It wasn't much, but at least it was work for Murray, which would be the sole producer of all the Ford wagon bodies for the next seven years.

At the dealers, the station wagons were never big sellers. They just hadn't caught on with the public. Sporting and well crafted as they looked, they were considered too expensive, too open to the elements, and took too much upkeep to think of using them as family cars. They appealed more to the wealthy and maybe a few travelers and explorers.

You weren't likely to see one on a road in Kansas or Nebraska. But you would probably see one in New England or Southern California, or if you took a vacation to Yellowstone or the Grand Canyon.

At Ford, the decision to keep producing such slow-sellers was never easy. They usually dropped a commercial model when yearly sales were less than a thousand. The 1932 station wagons came dangerously close to that limit. Sales were just one for every six Ford dealers in the U.S.

However, Edsel Ford, the company executive in charge of the model line, held the station wagon close to his heart. He kept it in production. Maybe it was because he wanted to help his old friend C.W. Avery and the Murray company stay afloat until times got better.

Meanwhile, Ford's Iron Mountain plant was surviving the lean years by producing dry-kiln hardwood. Although wood for passenger car bodies had all but disappeared, the plant continued to supply the wood to Mengel Body in Louisville to make the Ford station wagon body assemblies, and they also supplied the wood for Ford commercial bodies. Additionally, they were supplying wholesale hardwood for home flooring.

Norwegian-born Walter G. Nelson went to work at Ford Iron Mountain as a chemist in 1924, rising to become plant manager in 1936. "Over a period of years," he recalled in a 1952 interview, "the (car body) wood was gradually being eliminated, piece by piece. The pillars were changed to steel; the rails were changed to stampings."

Then, suddenly at the beginning of 1934, Iron Mountain got a lucky break! Mengel Body, which had produced the finished Ford station wagon wood parts from the beginning, had to give up the contract.

"The station wagon was taking hold," said Nelson, "and the (Ford) sales department was asking for increased production. Mengel couldn't keep up . . . so we were asked to do the job. We built the wood panels and shipped them to Murray for assembly." Nelson, who was a shop foremen at the time, recalled that Iron Mountain set up a

All photos in this chapter courtesy of the Henry Ford Museum Research Center, except where noted.

A new Murray-bodied Ford Station Wagon at a 1933 Stamping Division exhibit

Beyond a Murray Corporation exhibit of steel stampings at Ford's big 1933 Exposition show in Detroit is a crowd-pleasing new V-8 station wagon. Murray had just taken back from Baker-Raulang the job of building all the handcrafted Ford wood wagon bodies, a contract it would have for the next seven years. Led by C.W. Avery, the big Detroit firm produced parts and bodies for many American automakers. For more than two decades it supplied all the Ford station wagon metal stampings such as the cowls, floorpans, and rear fenders and furnished other parts for passenger and commercial vehicles like frames, fender, seat springs and body panels. During the thirties, the company built fully trimmed bodies for such special Ford passenger car types as the coupes, convertibles and victorias.

moving assembly line to mill its own hardwood, then join, glue, and sand the entire knocked down wood panels and parts for the '34 station wagon. The complete kits were built at the rate of about fifty per day. They were then shipped to Murray in Detroit where, along with the sheet metal stampings, they were assembled into complete bodies.

Lumber from the Ford hardwood forests around Iron Mountain was perfect for making high-quality automobile station wagon bodies. Even after all the Model T years, first growth maple, birch, ash, and basswood were still fairly plentiful. But, while just about every piece of green slab was good enough for the inside skeleton of a Model T sedan body, just seven to eight percent of kiln-dried maple planks were found suitable enough to go into a station wagon. That was after rejecting for knots, cracks, warps, end checking, and other defects. As for the panelling, Ford specified that it be, "cross-grained exterior birch plywood, good on both sides."

The late Dr. Tom Garrett, a Ford Sportsman authority, studied Iron Mountain body wood production and made a report in his *Seventy-One Society* newsletter: "The rough stock was first run through a planer to a given thickness. Then, through a tenoner, which would cut it to proper length and cut the tenons or 'fingers.' Parts were given an application of glue, assembled under pressure, and clamped until dry. The parts were then scroll-sawed to rough shape and run through a battery of shapers until completed. Most sanding was done by hand." The bare parts and body panels were sprayed with a fungicide to stop mold and mildew. They were then shipped to Murray.

Even as Ford station wagon sales increased, station wagon bodies remained just a small part of the Murray body building operations for Ford. In 1935, one of Murray's most profitable years, it produced for Ford, in addition to station wagon bodies, those of the three and five-window coupes, convertibles, and pickups.

Life was not getting any easier up north, as reported in a 1940 issue of *Ford News*:

"Iron Mountain was still furnishing Ford wood but work here had declined because the new passenger cars required even less of this material. By 1937, even the roof rib job was lost to the new steel top, and the plant was down to a skeleton crew making seat frames, truck platform racks, wood parts for sedan deliveries, and what had become their main occupation the manufacture of components for the station wagon."

Ford's head of purchasing A.M. Wibel squeezed every penny out of his suppliers, even Edsel's friend C.W. Avery.

It is noteworthy that Wibel figured the cost of bodies by the pound, with the breakdown for the 1936 station wagon built by Murray at .1822 cents. The '37 was slightly more at .1864 cents.

Including the Iron Mountain wood kits, Murray charged Ford $186.94 to assemble and finish a 1937 station wagon body with curtains. An additional $7.50 was tacked on for one with glass. Murray provided all the sheet metal stampings required for the 1937 wagon bodies, but the forged brackets and other parts came from two other companies — Benton Harbor Malleable, and United Brass & Aluminum Co. In a September 10, 1937, letter, Wibel reminded Avery that, "In connection with the manufacture of these bodies, Ford Motor Company reserves the right to supply all raw materials, purchased finish items, and interchangeable parts from other models."

In another letter to Avery on September 22, 1937, Wibel who would ordinarily order a couple of hundred, requested just fifty of the new 1938 bodies for the new model introduction show. Big body production changes were coming at Ford, car sales were generally down, and he was playing it close to the vest. ◆

"Station wagon wood had been built by Mengel Body at Louisville prior to 1934. Mengel couldn't keep up with the demand so wood panels were made at Iron Mountain and shipped to Murray for assembly." W.G. NELSON, MANAGER OF FORD NORTHERN MICHIGAN OPERATIONS

Iron Mountain's Walter G. Nelson

1933 FORD V-8 STATION WAGON Model 48-860
Production –1,654 with the standard 75 h.p. V-8,
and 359 with the 50 h.p. 4–cylinder engine

$590 Detroit

Body by Murray

It was all new from bumper-to-bumper, with rakish passenger car lines, classic heart-shaped grille, and fashionable front-opening "suicide doors." Times were tough but hotels and resorts catering to wealthy guests with a taste for the sporting lifestyle found it hard to resist the shapely 1933 Ford *Station Wagon*. Henry Ford was so pleased, he ordered one hand-lettered to pick up guests at his airport hotel in Dearborn.

1933 HAS SMART LINES

The new Ford *Station Wagon* is passenger car and bus, baggage and equipment carrier, camp car and delivery wagon. In any service, its smart lines and attractive two-tone maple panelling mark it as a vehicle of unusual distinction. It will seat eight, including driver. Tailgate serves as luggage deck. Rear and center seats are removable. Sides and rear can be enclosed . . . *1933 FORD COMMERCIAL CARS*

1934 FORD V-8 STATION WAGON Model 46-860
Production — 2,905 with 85 h.p. V-8,
95 with 50 h.p. 4-cylinder

$660 Detroit

Body by Murray

1934 GAINS POPULARITY

The Ford *Station Wagon* . . . has found wide acceptance with hotels, country clubs, camps, suburban estates, surveying crews, mining engineers, construction men, plantation overseers, sportsmen, Boy Scouts, and other organizations. Bus operators use it for "feeder" lines and during rush period overflow. The body is roomy and comfortable, built of hard maple finished in its natural color. Panelling is well ribbed for strength. Appearance is unusually smart. *1934 FORD COMMERCIAL CARS*

Discovered at the lodges and hunt clubs, the sporting Ford V-8 station wagons were gaining popularity at wealthy country homes and estates as owners bought them to impress friends. The new '34 models had slightly restyled front-ends and other changed details like dash panel and hubcap design.

The '34 wagon body had woodwork by Iron Mountain, with assembly and finish by Murray Corporation of America.

When Mengel Body of Louisville couldn't handle the 1934 job, for the first time Ford's Iron Mountain plant began supplying the finished station wagon body wood panels and parts to Murray Corporation. It was a job long overdue. Company management didn't think Iron Mountain had the skills. But their craftsmanship — as represented by the handsome panelling on this wagon, out on a nice Michigan summer day, proved to be first-rate! Iron Mountain went on to furnish all the beautiful woodwork for every Ford wagon until the plant closed in 1951.

COLORADO BOUND

At a Michigan train depot, some World War I disabled vets load their curtained '34 station wagon for a trip to a summer reunion in Colorado Springs. It was just the kind of use this ruggedly handsome V–8 was designed for. More than a car, but just as speedy out on the open road, it carried six easily with their extra baggage lashed onto the tailgate.

1933-34 FORD STATION WAGON
Specifications in general

CHASSIS & EQUIPMENT – 112-inch wheelbase. 50 h.p. 4-cyl. standard (1933), 85 h.p. V-8 engine standard (1934). Standard equipment includes 5.50x17 6-ply tires, right well fender with spare and fabric tire cover, and sideview mirror. Extra cost options include 75 h.p. V-8 engine (1933), metal tire cover, and factory installed left well fender.

BODY

Hard *maple* frame
Birch plywood panels
Basswood roof slats
Top fabric color is 48-866620 light *Brown* artificial leather

INTERIOR

Seats are fine Colonial-grain *Black-Brown* artificial leather. The 1933 instrument panel is painted *Winterleaf Brown;* 1934 Instrument panel is painted *Gray, Winterleaf Brown, Maroon,* or *Cordoba Gray. Tan* sliding side-curtains. Snap-on rear curtain. *Tan* rubber floor mats.

COLOR (hood and cowl)

CORDOBA GRAY or *MOUNTAIN BROWN,* with black wheels
BLACK fenders

Source:
1933-34 Ford Body Parts List
1933-34 Ford factory sales letters
1933-34 Ford sales literature

1933 Ford Station Wagon

The 1933-34 Ford *Station Wagon* bodies are identical except for the outside door handles (1933 handle is the same as 1929-32's) and subtle differences in cowl ventilator and tailgate detail. The side curtains stored neatly into the basswood slat ceiling on slide channels. Each unit turned out was a Murray masterpiece of wood panelling and joinery, tastefully fitted with simple hardware and fabric.

Left: A look at the well-tailored curtain detail of the '33-34 wagon body; the outside blind nuts painted body metal color; and the delicate furniturework of the tailgate. The roof is a smooth tan artificial leather specially produced at Ford's Highland Park plant.

A '33 Station Wagon pictured at Ford with early production "skirtless" fenders

The 1933-34 Ford body construction and details are nearly identical.

When Central High School in Los Angeles needed another seat in their '34 wagon to go on field trips, they just had a "caboose" tacked neatly on to the back.

A 1934 Ford Station Wagon at a desert rest stop in the search for oil.

A tribesman worker for the Arabian American Oil Company finds the running board of a hard-working '34 Ford *Station Wagon* a good resting spot in the morning heat. Equipped with balloon tires and strapped-on spares, the wagon belonged to an American survey team exploring what would become the fabulous oil fields of Saudi Arabia. Photo courtesy of ARAMCO

It didn't get any better in 1934 than touring the U.S. in a new Ford V-8 station wagon. The Steinhilber family from New York gets ready to move on from a roadside camping spot somewhere way out west.

"The new wagon attracted a lot of attention all across the country . . . whenever we would stop at a small town or gas station." BUDD STEINHILBER

Budd Steinhilber is an industrial designer who worked on the Tucker automobile project with his good friend Tucker Madawick (page 147). In the summer of 1934, Budd's father, "a *Ford Times* watercolor artist and perennial traveller," bought a new Ford station wagon direct from the factory in Detroit and took his family from their home in Woodstock, New York, on a 6,500 mile coast-to-coast camping adventure covering 21 states. They fitted the wagon with a large camp kitchen chest that fit snugly in the back, with the rear tailgate acting as the "kitchen table." Their first destination was the 1934 Chicago World's Fair. Budd remembers that they always carried an extra 5-gallon can of gas because "we never knew where the next gas station was going to be."

The snug wagon, Mom, and the Steinhilber kids

Budd Steinhilber (sitting on running board) with his mom, brother and sister, breaking camp with the family wagon near Cimmarron, New Mexico, in the summer of 1934.

—1935-36—

MOVIE WAGON

Crew and stars of the Ford-produced promotional film *"The Honeymoon V-8,"* featuring a new '35 *Roadster* and a starry eyed couple bound cross-country to the San Diego Fair, pose for publicity at the Rouge plant in Dearborn, Michigan. Their camera car is a sporty '35 Ford *Station Wagon* that has been neatly modified for the job with shooting platforms and such equipment as stabilizing rods stored under the running boards that were attached roof-to-ground when filming topside. Wood advertising panels fill in the side windows. Optional chrome wire wheels, roof-stashed spare, and whitewall tires make the outfit a real eye-catcher.

Finding a place on the tailgate for the spare tire was accomplished for the first time in 1935 by adding a compensating spring to assist raising and lowering.

1936 Ford spare tire mount with metal cover

One of the unworkable places tried for locating the 1935 spare tire mount

1935 FORD STATION WAGON Model 48-790
Production — 4,536

$670 Detroit

Body by Murray

To meet competition, Ford was forced to begin changing styling every year. The 1935 model established the look for all future Ford station wagons with the first streamlined horizontal slat body panel design, and the first with the tailgate-mounted spare. A well-executed production sample brought over to check the fit and finish of the Murray-built body is pictured at Ford Engineering in Dearborn, October 24, 1934. It is notable that the first automobile to officially cross the completely finished San Francisco Bay Bridge was a State of California '35 Ford *Station Wagon*.

A fender painted Cordoba Gray, the standard color for '35 Ford station wagons, is attached to a chassis at the Long Beach, California, assembly plant in February 1935.

Mechanics prepare 85 h.p. "flathead" V-8 truck (straight shift), and passenger car (bent shift) engines for assembly at Long Beach in 1935. Wagons received the passenger types.

An artist's view shows how the '35–36 side curtains stored in the roof on slide channels. With the rear seats removed and the tailgate lowered on covered drop chains, the wagon became a handy hauler for everything from ladders to lawnmowers. A patterned rubber mat and tailgate skid straps were nice touches to protect the finish. In June, 1936, an optional rear bumper became available for the first time on Ford station wagons.

1936 FORD STATION WAGON Model 68-790
Production – 7,044
    $670 Detroit   *Body by Murray*

"Safety glass will soon be available through production for rear doors and rear quarter panels of station wagons at $35.00 list extra. This glass fits in the regular curtain channels without interference with the standard curtains. The top and bottom is fastened by special channels, which are readily installed and removed, though not adjustable." FORD GENERAL SALES DEPARTMENT, APRIL 2, 1936

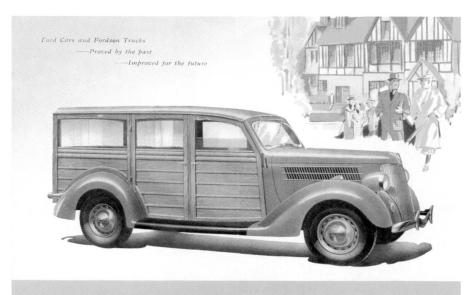

A UTILITY CAR FOR SHOOTING PARTIES

1936 English Ford ad, courtesy of the Bob Jones collection

A 1936 Ford 4-door sedan handsomely reworked into a longer-bodied custom "woodie."

The designer of this '36 Ford "woodie" had panelling ideas that appeared later on the Sportsman and '49 wagons.

Left: The rear styling of the special wood-panelled '36 Ford pictured above shows a distinct British flair. It is much like their popular station wagon-type "shooting brakes" of that era, used for hunting. Cleverly worked into the steel of the modified sedan body is a back window that opens, and a tailgate that lowers the same as a station wagon. Metal brackets reinforce key wood joints.

Even in 1936, people were finding ways to make regular Fords into their own kind of woodies. The one above may be the first with an all-steel body. And the first with wood panels over steel, like the future Ford *Sportsman* and '49–51 models. It was built by neatly extending the rear quarter section of a production '36 Ford *Deluxe Fordor Sedan* to give it more room inside, then very skillfully adding on the woodwork.

1936 Ford Station Wagon

1935–36 FORD STATION WAGON
Specifications in general

CHASSIS & EQUIPMENT — 112-inch wheelbase. 85 h.p. V-8 engine. Standard equipment includes 6.00 x 16 6-ply tires. Metal spare tire cover and lock available at extra cost.

BODY

Hard *Maple* frame
Birch plywood panels
Basswood roof slats
Top fabric color is 48-796620 *Brown* artificial leather.

INTERIOR

1935 seats are *Gray Brown Veal Grain* artificial leather. 1936 seats are *Brown Fine Colonial Grain* artificial leather trim. The 1935 instrument panel is *Metallic Taupe* (same as Cabriolet). 1936 instrument panel is *Benton Gray* (early), *Walnut Grain* (late). 1935 has *Tan* rubber floor mats front and rear. 1936 has *Benton Gray* rubber floor mats front and rear.

1935 BODY METAL COLOR

CORDOBA GRAY, with *Cordoba Gray* or *Medium Poppy Red* wheels.

1936 BODY METAL COLOR

CORDOBA TAN with wheels in same color.

Source:
1935–36 Ford factory sales letters
The Early Ford V-8, as Henry Built It
1935–36 Ford sales literature
1935–36 Ford Body Parts List

Sharing the same body cabinetry, the 1935-36 Ford station wagons had restyled maple framing with horizontal bar panelling. The front doors hinged again at the cowl and for the first time had roll-up glass windows. A pair of center seats folded forward so passengers could get to the three-passenger rear seat. In 1936 buyers were offered a choice of rear axles and chose the 3.54 ratio 3-to-1 over the "high-speed" options.

A 1936 Ford Station Wagon with the commercial exhibit at Ford's famous Rotunda showplace

CLASS OF 1936

All Ford station wagons were designated commercial vehicles until 1938. Here, in the summer of 1936 at the newly opened Ford Rotunda building in Dearborn, Michigan, a handcrafted *Station Wagon* model in standard *Cordoba Tan* color is exhibited with others in its class, including a pickup, sedan delivery, trucks, and panels. The soaring, gear-shaped Rotunda housed the Ford exhibit at the 1934 Chicago World's Fair and had been dismantled and rebuilt at Dearborn as what would become a landmark Ford visitor's center.

What thoughts must have run through a new car buyer's mind. Whether to buy an ordinary '37 Ford, or wow the neighbors with one of these varnished maple beauties!

—1937—

Professionals found that the Ford station wagons, with their incomparable good looks and fine wood construction, were good for business. A contractor who drove something like this was more likely to build a quality house. Surveyors, photographers and geologists bought them because they projected a successful image and were ideal for carrying sensitive equipment. Real estate salesmen used them to give tours.

A truck and *Deluxe*-equipped *Station Wagon* are pictured in the commercial section of the Ford exhibit at the big Michigan State Fair September 7, 1937.

Left: An appealing trio, a *Deluxe*-equipped Ford *Station Wagon* for the estate, a sporty softtop *Club Cabriolet* for Mom, and a snazzy *Deluxe Fordor Touring Sedan* for Junior in college. The picture was taken at the Bloomfield Hills, Michigan, horse show June 3, 1937.

A worker sands a beautifully-crafted maple and birch station wagon front door on the assembly line at the Ford Iron Mountain plant in August, 1937. The doors were the most critical in building a station wagon body. They had to fit and hang perfectly in the frame.

Right: Iron Mountain produced the Ford station wagon woodwork, including loose pieces, assembled doors, quarter panels, tailgate and seat frames. The un–varnished "kit" was then sent to Murray for final body assembly and finish.

The completed Iron Mountain '37 station wagon body wood, ready for assembly by Murray

1937 FORD STATION WAGON Model 78-790A
Production – 9,304 (about half with curtains)

$755 Detroit

Body by Murray

1937 FORD STATION WAGON
Specifications in general

CHASSIS & EQUIPMENT – 112-inch wheelbase. 85 h.p., or 60 h.p. V-8 optional. Standard-equipment includes 6.00x16 6-ply tires, and spare tire with metal cover and lock.

BODY

Hard *Maple* frame
Birch plywood panels
Basswood roof slats
Top fabric color is 78-796620 *Brown* artificial leather.

INTERIOR

Seats are *Brown Fine Colonial Grain* artificial leather. Instrument panel is *American Walnut-grain* (same as '37 convertible models). Roll-up side-curtains. Safety glass inserts optional. *Benton Gray* rubber floor mats.

BODY METAL COLOR

AUTUMN BROWN, or any of these standard Truck and Commercial Car colors by dealer order only: *Black, Gull Grey, Vermillion Red, Coach Maroon Bright, Bright Vineyard Green*, and *Washington Blue*. Wheels to match.

Source:
1937 Ford factory sales letters
1937 Ford sales literature
1937 Ford Body Parts List

While basically the same architecture as the 1935-36 models, the '37 Ford *Station Wagon* had different maple frame rails at the belt line, below the windows. They were now smooth, instead of double-shaped as before. In place of the old leather-covered tailgate chains were jointed rods. The raised rear seat platform was now rounded at the corners to save ankles.

A steel framed glass rear window was a new feature on '37 models. Side curtains came standard, with glass optional. Rear bumper was now standard.

A '36 station wagon accessory package offered in mid-summer sold so well that it was promoted heavily for 1937. So many '37 wagons were ordered with these features that they were designated "Deluxe" models with "790-B" on the Murray body tag. As pictured here, the 1937 "Deluxe" has a banjo spoke steering wheel, Deluxe dash, and dual wipers, etc. The regular wagons have Standard steering wheel and features.

Visitors to the Ford Rotunda in Dearborn try seating for eight. Sliding glass side windows were optional on the new '37 wagon models.

DELUXE OPTION

A *Deluxe Accessory Group* has been specified for the *Station Wagon*, effective at once, consisting of the following: chrome wheel bands, tandem windshield wipers, Deluxe steering wheel, glove compartment lock and handle, sun visor, and dome light. FORD GENERAL SALES DEPARTMENT JUNE 9, 1936

Ford began promoting the new station wagon as more than just a utility vehicle, but as a second family car that would look good in your driveway. By 1937, radio, spotlight, heater and defroster, locking gas cap, and white sidewall tires were some of the optional accessories on station wagons.

Marmon-Herrington offered its first 4-wheel-drive equipment on light duty Fords in 1937. Some of the station wagon models converted that year stand high and ready for work outside the company's plant in Indianapolis.

"Marmon-Herrington All-Wheel-Drive Fords get their superior performance on hills, in mud, sand, dirt or snow from the added traction of four wheels, all pulling and pushing at the same time. With live, grasping, climbing traction on all wheels it is positively amazing what these vehicles will do!" THE MARMON-HERRINGTON CO.

For a Marmon-Herrington-equipped 1937 Ford station wagon, deep snow was all in a day's work. The famous 4-wheel drive was designed for wherever the going was really tough.

MARMON HERRINGTON

No Ford woodie book would be complete without mention of the 4-wheel drive Marmon-Herrington's and the two men who formed the legendary company in 1931. Walter C. Harmon was a founder of the Marmon Motor Company whose Marmon "Wasp" won the first Indy "500" race in 1911. Colonel Arthur W. Herrington was an ex-military engineer who designed all-wheel drive vehicles. They saw a need for go-anywhere vehicles and in 1935 introduced the first big 4-wheel drive Ford trucks. This was followed in 1937 with their first light duty Ford models, including the station wagon. By 1938 they were offering fifty-four Ford models with 4-wheel-drive running gear. They specialized in equipping Fords from 1935 to 1948 and are still converting commercial trucks to all-wheel drive today.

Col. Harrington demonstrates a 4-wheel-drive '37 Ford station wagon.

A Marmon-Herrington 1938 Ford Deluxe Station Wagon, *typically equipped with 7.50x15 tires.*

In a typical light Ford Marmon-Herrington conversion like a station wagon, a new front driving axle with longitudinal springs was installed along with a transfer case. Changes were also made to the steering. Rugged high-clearance wheels and balloon tires replaced the regular equipment.

Ford woodies were at their best taking adventurous Americans to places they'd never seen before.

Rustic Glen Stage Company '38 Ford V-8 station wagons bring wide-eyed sightseers down from the summit of New Hampshire's lofty Mt. Washington. From the beginning, resorts and lodges found the rustic wood-panelled 3-seat Ford wagons helped bring in guests looking for a memorable stay.

—1938-39—

The first new '39 Ford Deluxe Station Wagon shown in Detroit

Ready for the crowd, a '39 wagon stands gleaming on the floor of the Ford commercial line exhibit at Detroit's Convention Hall, shortly before dealer introductions in November, 1938. Topping the list of 1939 Ford selling points were the safer new hydraulic brakes — something Henry Ford had stubbornly resisted but finally gave in to because his old cable-operated mechanicals were killing sales.

The 1938 Ford models were the first designed completely by Edsel and his chief stylist E.T. "Bob" Gregorie, without the usual help from outside studios. The custom-looking Ford station wagon was now recognized for how it was actually used. It was elevated this year from the commercial line. From here on all of these by-now much admired utilities would be classified as "passenger cars."

Left: From the back, the cleanly-styled '38-39 wagons looked the same. The spare was moved inside. The tailgate was now opened with a center handle.

The 1938 Ford wagon body(pictured) and 1939 models have spare tire mounted inside.

1938 FORD STATION WAGON Model 790
Production – 6,944

$825 Detroit

Body by Murray

1939 FORD DELUXE STATION WAGON

To many a country home owner, the *Deluxe Ford V-8 Station Wagon* is almost a necessity. It is appropriately styled to serve in settings that call for beauty, and built to conform with strict Ford standards of reliability and long life. As a passenger vehicle, it seats eight including the driver — and is quickly converted into utility hauling unit by removing rear and center seats. The handsome body is hard *maple* in natural finish. 85 h.p. Ford V-8 engine. Hydraulic brakes. *1939 FORD PASSENGER CARS*

The finely-crafted, modern-looking 1939 Ford *Station Wagon* was high-society's latest status symbol. The '39 Ford front-end design reflected the designers' keen interest in boating. Edsel Ford liked "pointy shapes." So, like his new Lincoln-Zephyr's of this period, chief stylist Bob Gregorie adapted the streamlined "cut-through-water" boat prow look to great effect.

1939 FORD DELUXE STATION WAGON Model 79
Production – 5,721 (with glass)
27 with side curtains

$925 Detroit

Body by Murray

The interior rear door detail of a '39 Ford Deluxe Station Wagon showing an early use of gum-wood panel veneer to give an artistic darker-grained two-tone effect against the lighter maple frame. Also, the door handle (fits '39-40) borrowed from the '33-34 Roadster. Brown-finished interior metal trim detail was common to all 1929-48 Ford wagons.

Right: An early Ford station wagon ad in color captures a scene at a modern train station. The featured '39 *Deluxe* depicts a brown top. This would be common to all Ford wagons 1933-48.

Below: For 1939, Ford offered a distinctly-styled, more commercial-looking, *Standard* model station wagon as a lower-priced option to the *Deluxe*. Just $85 separated the two types. Buyers recognized more value in the fancier of the two, which had such niceties as twin wipers and visors, bright windshield trim instead of rubber, and leather seats. So it was the better seller by far.

TWO NEW FORD V-8
Station Wagons FOR 1939

EACH COMBINING BEAUTY WITH UTILITY

1939 FORD STANDARD STATION WAGON *Model 79*
Production – 2,203 with glass, 315 with side curtains.

$840 Detroit

Body by Murray

1938-39 FORD STATION WAGON
Specifications in general

CHASSIS & EQUIPMENT — 112-inch wheelbase. 85 h.p. V-8. Standard equipment includes 6.00x16 6-ply tires, with spare cover on *Deluxe* models.

BODY

Hard *Maple* frame
Birch plywood panels
Basswood roof slats
Top fabric for 1938 is M2600-E *Green*, or M2600-D *Brown* artificial leather. 1939 models are M-2600-D *Brown* artificial leather.

INTERIOR

1938 seats are *Brown Fine Colonial Grain* artificial leather. '39 *Deluxe* seats have *Tan Genuine Leather* seat cushions with backs trimmed in artificial leather. '39 *Standard* is upholstered in *Tan* artificial leather throughout. 1938 instrument panel is straight *Walnut-grain* finish. '39 *Standard* is *Antique-grain Mahogany*. '39 *Deluxe* instrument panel is *Golden Birch-grain* finish. 1938 rubber floor mats are *Benton Gray*. '39 rubber floor mats are dark brown.

1938 BODY METAL COLOR

DESERT TAN, BRIGHT VINEYARD GREEN. DARTMOUTH GREEN, or any *Deluxe* passenger car color by special dealer order.

1939 DELUXE BODY METAL COLORS

COACH MAROON BRIGHT or *WREN TAN* with optional *Black, Jefferson Blue, Dartmouth Green, Gull Gray, Cloudmist Gray* (after 4-1-39), and *Folkestone Gray.*

1939 STANDARD METAL COLORS

WREN TAN, with *Black, Jefferson Blue,* and *Gull Gray* optional

The all-new Ford station wagon body for 1938 was also shared by the two new *Standard* and *Deluxe* models for 1939. Notable differences inside were the driving compartments and seat stitching designs. The 1939 *Deluxe* rear rubber floor mats were also more tailored. A new feature on *Deluxe* models was the arm rest on the two-passenger center seat.

Sources:
1938-39 Ford factory sales letters
1938-39 Ford sales literature
1938-39 Ford Body Parts Lists

1938 Ford Deluxe Station Wagon

The 1938 Ford wagons were the first with the spare tire mounted inside. A simple canvas-type cover came standard.

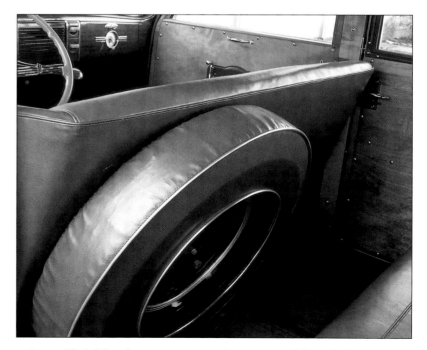

An artificial leather-type spare tire cover, with stainless ring came standard on the more expensive 1939 Deluxe models.

Mom and Dad camping in style with their trusty '39 Ford Standard Station Wagon

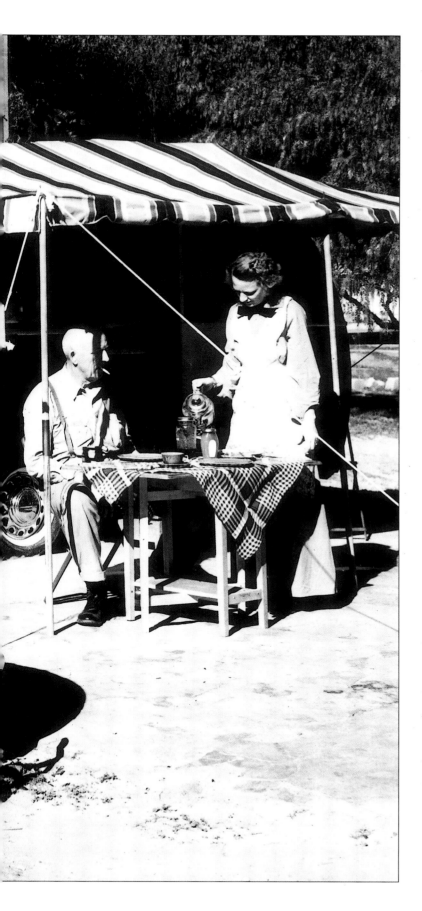

ALL THE COMFORTS OF HOME

Mr. and Mrs. J.D. Hill enjoy breakfast relaxing at a California roadside park with their snug "cabin trailer." It was becoming a common scene as more Americans were choosing the Ford wagon for work or play. The Hills' new wagon provides good '39 *Standard* details such as the light-colored *(Brown)* top, and the body-color rear door piano hinge and top rain gutter. The center bumper grille guard was a popular aftermarket add on.

FAMOUS HOLLY WOODIES

The popularity of Ford woodie wagons as the "in" cars among Hollywood movie stars and other celebrities probably hit its peak from 1937 to 1941. Those were also the years of some of the great classic movies like, *"Gone With the Wind," "The Wizard of Oz,"* and *"The Grapes of Wrath."*

In a 1941 news article, writer Sheridan Keane said Katherine Hepburn was the film star who really made Hollywood so station wagon conscious. "Having come from Connecticut, she found those cars of the varnished wood bodies no novelty at all. But Hollywood gaped at her wagon (a 1932 Ford) . . . and within ten years the station wagon had become the smartest Hollywood buggy."

Clark Gable liked to get away from Hollywood to go fishing and hunting and had a succession of Ford station wagons, purchasing his first one in 1937.

According to Keane, Gable and his wife, Carole Lombard, used the Ford to carry their camping and hunting equipment, including racks for guns and clay pigeons. "They usually spend their vacations at a ranch near the California-Mexico border," she wrote, " but out in the open they sleep in the wagon in preference to staying in hotels that furnish much less privacy."

Character actor Wallace Beery was one of the biggest admirers of Fords and Lincolns in Hollywood. He bought lots of them, including a 1932 station wagon and a '39 Deluxe. In 1941, he bought one of the jazzy new Mercury station wagons that, "opened up like a fisherman's paradise," said Keane in awe. "The back end is the rod-and-reel department. And, because he goes fishing so often, he doesn't bother to take the stuff out!"

Myrna Loy, star of *"The Thin Man"* series and other hits, was another station wagon owner. She owned a lime grove in Southern California and bought the Ford so her gardener could deliver limes to market in style. Her wagon was well known for the green limes painted on the doors.

Other film notables with Ford wagons during this era included Bette Davis, who tooled around town with her two Scotties hanging their heads out of the open windows; leading man Robert Taylor, who used his around the ranch to haul feed for his horses; and Frank Morgan who's door insignia was a life preserver with crossed Navy flags.

Joan Bennett's Ford wagon had the inscription *"Benmeldi"* on its doors, a contraction of Bennett and the names of her two young daughters Melinda and Diana. She chose it to foil autograph seekers who had learned how to find stars by the various signs on their wagon doors.

Reporter Keane noted that during this same period many movie directors, particularly those who lived on farms in the San Fernando Valley, also owned Ford or Mercury station wagons.

She said that King Vidor, Gregory Ratoff, and Mervyn LeRoy were among those who used them as portable offices, driving them right onto the movie sound stages to conduct business in, and interview bit players.

When actor Don Ameche was coming down with pneumonia while filming *"Down Argentine Way,"* he had his new Ford station wagon rolled onto the stage. With his wife nursing him back to health, he slept and ate in his prized wagon for three straight nights until he was well enough to go back before the cameras.

Mickey Rooney, who starred in *"Young Tom Edison,"* filmed at Henry Ford's Greenfield Village in Dearborn, sported around Hollywood in a '39 Deluxe model, a gift of the famous automaker. ◆

Right: **Handsome leading man Clark Gable was known for his fine taste in cars and was one of Hollywood's biggest Ford woodie fans, enjoying them for hunting and fishing at places like Oregon's Rogue River. He is pictured with his first — a travel-equipped '37 just picked up from Hall Motor Company in Culver City, California.**

Clark Gable takes a break from filming "Saratoga" to buy a sporting new '37 Ford station wagon.

"The old Iron Mountain foreman told me they had one crew kept busy on special jobs that went to celebrities and events — hand-rubbing the gloss off the varnished bodies to get a higher-quality look." CLIFF HELLING

Right: Seasoned character actor and sportsman Wallace Beery with his '39 Ford *Deluxe Station Wagon* on a snowy fishing trip to Jackson Lake, Wyoming.

Below: Paramount's Allan Jones gets one last publicity shot before putting *Chief* in the trailer and heading for shady mountain trails in his new '39 *Deluxe Station Wagon.* Jones was just one of many Hollywood celebrities who found these popular Fords a good way to take to the road.

Two old fishing pals and their trusty Ford wagon

Allan Jones with his new '39 Ford Deluxe Station Wagon *at Bel Aire Stables*

Ah! The smell of varnished wood and leather! Star of radio and film, comedian Jack Benny finds his nicely-equipped '39 Ford Deluxe wagon a good place to relax before stepping in front of the cameras for a scene with Fred Allen in "Love Thy Neighbor."

Film star Robert Montgomery off stage with his smart new '37 Ford Station Wagon during the filming of "Ever Since Eve."

1940

BODY BY IRON MOUNTAIN

1951

AN ALL-FORD BEAUTY!
the 1940 model

"Little Oxford is definitely gentry and definitely county. It prides itself on not being suburban. Yet it is not completely rural . . . There are fast daily trains for the commuter and an accessible airport for the air minded . . . It is famous for its many estates, ranging from five acres to a thousand . . . "

So wrote the author Faith Baldwin in her popular 1939 romantic novel *Station Wagon Set.* She laid her scene for the fictional place, Little Oxford, from a composite of the many places she knew "on Long Island, in Westchester and Connecticut, and in Jersey and Pennsylvania."

It was not a story of station wagons but of the people who could afford to own them — like the Pallisters who had "the biggest estate and the highest stone wall" in Little Oxford.

As portrayed in her book, the Ford station wagon had become a true American status symbol. No longer just a utility vehicle to haul people and equipment, it had been elevated from Ford's commercial line to the top end of the passenger class.

"She left the car at the station and saw Bill Niles on the platform . . . She saw the girl with him — the girl who had sung last night, who had sent Dave away from her. She was with Niles, clinging to his arm, laughing up into his face . . . and boarding the train with him . . . "

Far up in the north woods at the big Ford lumber operations of Iron Mountain, Michigan, manager Walter Nelson was scratching to get more work for his men.

There had always been a feeling of insecurity here, as far as a man's job was concerned. It was usually caused by the

Left: A gateman at Henry Ford's historic Greenfield Village in Dearborn admires a brand-new '40 Ford *Deluxe Station Wagon.* The first wagons with bodies completely built by Ford's own Iron Mountain plant, these beauties had it all! Handsome styling, leather seats, sealed-beam headlights, column shift, hydraulic brakes — all for less than a thousand dollars.

seasonal two to three month summer layoff resulting from the change-over in Dearborn to tool up for the new Ford models. And now, with the car bodies being nearly all steel, except for station wagon body panels, there was even less wood being used.

"In 1938 and 1939, there were only a few sticks of wood left in the passenger job," Nelson recalled. "To all intents and purposes, you might say that wood, as far as passenger jobs were concerned, was discontinued."

Meanwhile, there were rumblings and rumors down in Dearborn that Murray's longtime relationship with Ford purchasing was beginning to crack.

In March of that year, the department's head, A.M. Wibel, sent a strong letter to C.W. Avery, president of Murray Corporation, about the high prices quoted to build the current production of Ford station wagon bodies — and about Murray's continuing labor problems. He also replied to Avery's complaint about "the poor quality" of the Ford-made soybean-based varnish provided for use on the 1939 models.

"You state," wrote Wibel, "that you had no trouble during 1938 with varnish on the station wagon. You are correct. We have had some difficulty in making a varnish that would satisfactorily dry for you. When the job was made (in 1932) by Baker-Raulang Company, of Cleveland, it called for a four hour air dry which they brushed on, and we had no complaints whatever from the field. When you took the job over (in 1933), the station wagons were finished in a different manner and the varnish that we had been furnishing did not work in your different method. You now have the privilege of getting the varnish on the outside."

At the time of Wibel's caustic letter to Murray, Ford had completed a huge new Press Steel building at its colossal Rouge Plant in Dearborn where all the company's car bodies would now be made. Briggs was already out of the picture. Murray Corporation of America, other than designing, stamping parts for and building station wagon bodies for Ford, was down to providing front-end sheet metal stampings for the new Mercury, and frames, seat springs, and specialty fender stampings for the commercial line. (Still, their Ford business was twice what it was in 1936.) Beyond Murray's trouble with Ford purchasing, it was facing the gathering clouds of labor unrest.

Murray's mounting problems would prove to be a big break for Iron Mountain. "At that time," recalled Walter Nelson, "our employment was down to a thousand people . . . Murray had been plagued by strikes, which hampered Ford Motor Company. Mr. Sorensen (Ford production chief) and the others in Dearborn decided to do the body construction work themselves."

Nelson was called down to Dearborn. They discussed whether his shops at Iron Mountain, which already turned out the finished panels and parts for the Ford station wagons, had the ability and space to assemble the complete bodies.

To assess the possibilities, Nelson and two of his key men, were soon visiting the Murray plant, picking up whatever information they could. Back on the lawn at the Dearborn Inn where they were staying, they would sit in the evenings laying out the various operations and discussing them with George Scarlet, the Dearborn liaison man to Iron Mountain.

"Their intent at that time was to have us build just the shell and then ship it to the various plants for trimming," said Nelson. "I asked Mr. Sorensen for the privilege of doing the job in its entirety at Iron Mountain. Some of the others were reluctant to give us any part of that because, as they said, we had nothing but wood butchers up here and knew nothing of trim operations such as sewing, cutting, painting, varnishing and so on. Mr. Sorensen said, "Let's give them the complete job. We'll send some people up there from the various trim operations and get them started. There's no reason why they can't do the job."

With Edsel Ford's backing, Nelson and his men installed the complete station wagon body building operations at Iron Mountain. Essentially, this amounted to starting with a rough log and turning it into a completely assembled, trimmed, and finished body ready for shipment.

Ford pulled the wagon job from Murray but left intact their contract to continue supplying Mercury hood and fender stampings, certain commercial and truck stampings, and station wagon stampings like cowls, floorpans, and rear fenders.

When Iron Mountain took over the station wagon body building in the late summer of 1939, the morale of the workers soared. "The quality of the workmanship on the station wagon body was considerably improved," reported *Ford Iron Mountain News.* "Now, men in the woodworking

"In 1939 Murray was having a series of strikes which hurt production so assembly of station wagon bodies was transferred to Iron Mountain . . ." W.G. NELSON, MANAGER OF FORD NORTHERN MICHIGAN OPERATIONS

shops who previously saw the last of their efforts when the wood parts were loaded into boxcars for shipment to Detroit, see the results of their efforts in the finished product on the final assembly line. As a consequence, they have taken added interest in their work. This pride is evidenced in better-fitting and better-fashioned body parts."

"They asked me to set the operation up at seventy-five a day," said Nelson. "Before that year was over, we were building something like one hundred station wagons a day."

Iron Mountain had gotten into production handily and was actually building the units cheaper than Murray had. By the first week of August the plant completed two hundred station wagon bodies. They were for shipment to assembly plants for the company's first introductory showings of the new 1940 Ford models across the nation on September 29, 1939. Soon after, buyers from sunny Santa Barbara, to toney Southampton, would have an opportunity to visit their Ford dealer and drive home one of these maple-framed beauties. ◆

"When they drove up, Tony's car was prominent in the crowded parking space. There was plenty of noise and plenty of light. There were couples sitting in the parked cars. The sound of music came blaring out at them. Pete's lips tightened. But Thalia's eyes danced. This was different. This was fun." FAITH BALDWIN, STATION WAGON SET

All photos in this chapter courtesy of the Henry Ford Museum Research Center, except where noted.

1940 FORD DELUXE STATION WAGON Model 01A79-B
Production — 8,114 with 85 h.p. V-8
354 with 95 h.p. V-8

$950 Detroit

Body by Ford, Iron Mountain

"It is interesting to observe hand production of a wood body for a modern automobile. Probably no other automobile model requires in its manufacture the amount of experienced hand labor expended in the finishing of every hardwood Ford V-8 Station Wagon. Here, one finds hand craftsmanship raised to its highest level of efficiency." FORD NEWS, 1940

BUILT WITH PRIDE

Just assembled Ford station wagon bodies are masked for the first coat of varnish at Iron Mountain. Labor problems at Murray, the longtime supplier of these hand-built types forced the Company to build the 1940 models here — and all those to the end of 1951.

At this point on the moving assembly line, the furniture-quality body woodwork has been sanded, the metal cowl primed, floorpan and wheel housings painted, and the tailgate and interior hardware installed. Factory instructions specified the 1940 *Deluxe* models to have "select grain hard *maple* or *birch* with high varnish rub." The Standards were to have one framing wood only: "natural finished hard maple." Both would get three coats of exterior varnish, with sanding between.

Hand sanded to a "piano finish," 1940 Iron Mountain station wagon bodies are prepared for varnish.

Beautifully crafted Standard model Ford Station Wagon bodies at Dearborn assembly April 29, 1940

NEW GUMWOOD PANELS

Finished 1940 Ford bodies with the latest *Gumwood* panelling arrive at the end of the paint dryer line at the Dearborn, Michigan, assembly plant. The darker-colored softwood veneer, from the *"Red Gumwood"* tree of the Southeastern U.S., was a new styling idea to add variety to the line. It was used at random with the regular blonde *Birch* on both *Standard* and *Deluxe* bodies. Stained lightly for consistent color, the exotic-grained panels helped sales and became a regular wagon feature.

THE FINISH LINE

Iron Mountain shipped the finished 1940 station wagon bodies to Ford assembly plants which painted the primed metal work. The district sales offices decided how many wagons in which colors and types they wanted for their area dealers, who also placed special orders for customers. *Maroon* was the most popular color chosen for the '40 *Deluxe*.

On the assembly line the wagon body was dropped on a V–8 passenger chassis, color-matched to a *Standard* or *Deluxe* front-end, and "factory-equipped" with such ordered extras as rear axle ratios, radio, side view mirrors, and whitewalls. Of the 18 Ford assembly plants in the U.S., the biggest 1940 wagon producers were Dearborn, Michigan; Edgewater, New Jersey; Richmond, California; and Chicago, Illinois — in that order.

1940 FORD STATION WAGON BODY
Specifications in general

CHASSIS & EQUIPMENT — 112-inch wheelbase. 85 h.p. V-8 engine. *Deluxe* model standard equipment includes 6.00x16 6-ply tires, spare tire cover and lock, dual wipers, visors and horns.

BODY

Deluxe has select grain hard *Maple* or *Birch* body with "high varnish rub." *Standard* has natural finish hard *Maple* body. *Gumwood* or *Birch* plywood panels. *Basswood* roof slats. Top fabric color is M2600-G *Brown* artificial leather.

INTERIOR

1940 DELUXE

Seat facings are upholstered in *Brown Spanish-grain genuine leather*, balance in artificial leather. Instrument panel is *Monaida Maroon* upper section, and *Copper Sand Metallic,* lower section. *Taupe* or *Black* rubber floor mats.

1940 STANDARD

Seats are *Brown* artificial leather. Instrument panel is *Briarwood Brown. Taupe* or *Black* rubber floor mats.

DELUXE BODY METAL COLORS

Black, Lyon Blue, Cloud Mist Gray, Folkestone Gray, Yosemite Green, Mandarin Maroon, Garnet Maroon

STANDARD BODY METAL COLORS

Black, Lyon Blue, Cloud Mist Gray

Source:
1940 Ford and Mercury Body Parts List
1940 Ford factory sales letters
1940 Ford sales literature

The 1940 Ford station wagon body was not just the first completely built by Iron Mountain but, fittingly, one-of-a-kind. The big difference from the side view was the reshaped roof line, the re-designed rear quarter panels, and the middle doors which were now hinged at the center post. Glass was now standard all around. The *Deluxe* front seat had the same sew style as the convertible model, and was now adjustable. The photo at the right shows the first pre-production body on a '39 chassis at Ford Engineering.

1940 Ford Deluxe Station Wagon

Nothing too fancy, just an all-business '40 Ford Standard Station Wagon set up to haul the surveying equipment of the Los Angeles Department of Power and Water.

1940 FORD STANDARD STATION WAGON Model 01A79-A
Production – 3,255 with 85 h.p., and 2 with 60 h.p.

$875 Detroit

Body by Ford, Iron Mountain

*Hollywood leading man Tyrone Power, with his new '41 Ford Super Deluxe
Station Wagon, as pictured in* Ford News *magazine. That year he starred
in "Blood and Sand." His well-documented wagon is now owned by Joe
Caputo of New York.*

-1941·42-

1941 FORD DELUXE STATION WAGON Model 11A79-A
Production – 8,128 (including 2,012 assembled in Canada)

$965 Detroit

Body by Ford, Iron Mountain

NEW FOR 1941

The *Super Deluxe Station Wagon* for 1941 carries even farther the tradition of smart styling and all round utility that has put Ford units of this type on many of the finest estates. As a passenger vehicle it seats eight. Front seat adjustable. Windows and windshield are Safety Glass. Doors and tailgate can be locked. A *Deluxe Station Wagon* is available at lower cost. *1941 FORD SALES BROCHURE*

A Wisconsin saddle horse farm used this '41 Ford *Deluxe Station Wagon,* and a companion '41 Ford bus, to carry polo players and staff to games. Lower-priced with plainer trim, the *Deluxe* wagons are quickly identified by the omitted *"Super Deluxe"* fender emblem. About a third of them were assembled by Ford-Canada for the British war effort.

1941 FORD SUPER DELUXE STATION WAGON Model 11A79-B   *$1,265 Detroit*   *Body by Ford, Iron Mountain*
Production – 9,485

Above: Everything about the Ford station wagon was new for 1941, including new front-end styling and a new body design to fit the longer new 114-inch wheelbase. One of the first of these good-looking models is pictured at a Ford Rotunda exhibit in Dearborn during the public debut of the new '41 line in late September, 1940.

The nifty artwork on a Louisville, Kentucky, florist's '41 Ford Super Deluxe Station Wagon

★ **The Smart Station Wagon** is a new **Mercury** body type. Front end and driver's compartment follow the sedan styling. Choice of tan, blue or red leather upholstery Large luggage capacity. White sidewall tires extra.

Mercury 8

NEW STATION WAGON★ has body of selected maple and birch. Holds up to 8 passengers. Genuine leather upholstery available in your choice of tan, blue or red.

1941 MERCURY STATION WAGON Model 19A79
Production – 2,143

$1,141 Detroit

Body by Ford, Iron Mountain

Ford introduced the Mercury nameplate for 1939 but it wasn't until 1941 that the station wagon was ready – to coincide with the shared new-style Ford body.

Left: Ford designers wanted the sporty new Mercury wagons to make a big splash. They did! For the first time buyers could chose from several selections of body panelling, and have their paint choice color-coordinated with the leather seats, and top fabric. In ads, the wagons had moved on from meeting the train – to meeting the plane.

STATION WAGON NEW TO MERCURY LINE

A brand-new body type, the *Station Wagon* finds new duties for the Mercury's powerful and economical engine. Front-end and driver's compartment are in sedan style. Body is framed in *maple* with *birch* panels, *gum* optional. Seats may be arranged for three, five, six or eight passengers, with plenty of room for luggage or other heavy loads. *1941 FORD PASSENGER CARS*

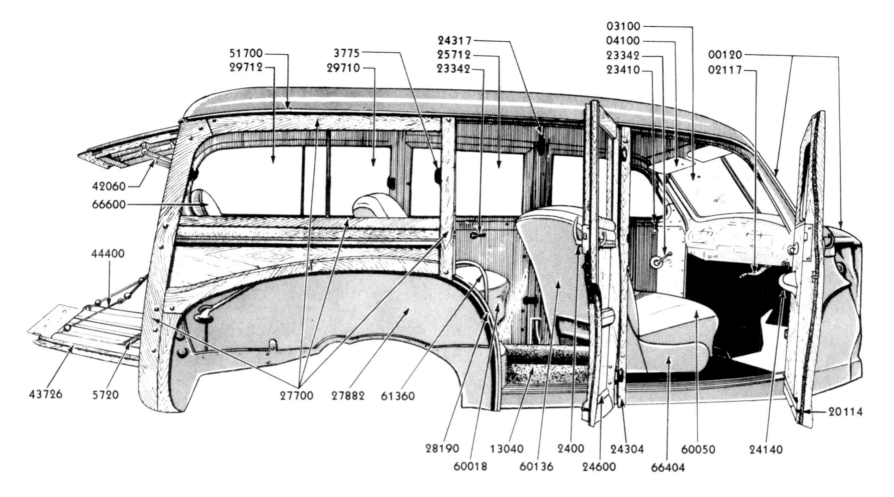

1941-42 FORD -MERCURY STATION WAGONS
Specification in general

CHASSIS & EQUIPMENT – Ford has 114-inch wheelbase. 90 h.p. V-8 engine. Mercury has 118-inch wheelbase. 95 h.p. V-8 engine. '41-42 Ford tires are 6.00x16 6-ply. '41-42 Mercury tires are 6.50x16 6-ply. Spare tire, cover, and lock is standard.

BODY

Maple framing. '41-42 Ford panels are *Birch* or *Gumwood*. '41 Mercury panels are *Brown-finished Gumwood, Brown-finished Birch, Chrome-finished Gumwood,* or *Chrome-finished Birch.* '42 Mercury panels are *Birch* or *Gumwood*. *Basswood* roof slats. Top fabric color is M2600-G *Brown* artificial leather (Mercury tops were often color-coordinated to match body metal color).

INTERIOR

'41 Ford *Super Deluxe* seats are *Light* or *Dark Tan genuine leather.* '41 *Deluxe* seats are *Dark Tan coarse-grain Moleskin* artificial leather or *Light Tan fine grain* artificial leather. '41 Mercury seat cushion faces are *Tan, Red,* or *Blue genuine leather.* Balance of trim is artificial leather. '42 Mercury seats are *Tan, Red,* or *Blue genuine leather.* '41 Ford *Super Deluxe* instrument panel is *Sequoia-grain* finish. '41 *Deluxe* instrument panel is *crackle Mahogany-grain.* '41 Mercury instrument panel is combination *Rosemont Beige* and *Gray-Elm grain.* '42 Mercury instrument panel is *Light Silver Walnut Grain* or *Mahogany Sequoia-grain.*

An all-new, re-designed 1941 station wagon body would be the same one produced for all 1941-48 Ford-Mercury models. Longer, with door bottom rails flared to conceal the running boards, the design featured new front door quarter window vents and rear quarter panels shaped to fit the new-style fenders.

1941 METAL COLORS

Black, Harbor Gray, Cayuga Blue, Lochaven Green, Mayfair Maroon (Ford *Super Deluxe* only), *Palisade Gray* (Ford *Deluxe* only). Also for 1941 Mercury: *Capri Blue Metallic* and *Cotswold Gray Metallic.* Wheels same as body colors.

1942 METAL COLORS

Black, Florentine Blue, Newcastle Gray, Niles Blue Green, Fathom Blue, Moselle Maroon, (plus for 1942 Mercury, *Village Green* and *Phoebe Gray Metallic*).

Source: 1941 Ford and Mercury Body Parts List; 1942 Ford and Mercury Body Parts List; 1941-42 Ford factory sales letters

---

Right: The handsome 1942 Ford station wagons (and Mercurys) were the last for the duration of the war. Considering the short production time because of the conflict, a fair number were built. Officially, only the *Super Deluxe* Ford models were offered, though assembly records show that 567 of the *"Deluxe"* type were produced – probably for the military.

Drivers with their "Publicos" of all makes wait for train passengers at Arecibo, Puerto Rico in 1942. Most preferred Ford station wagons over any other kind of taxi.

A brand-new '41 Ford Super Deluxe Station Wagon takes on an overload of Puerto Rican passengers, including one tied on the tailgate.

Jack Delano, one of the well known photographer's assigned by the Farm Security Administration to document the plight of the American worker during the Depression, captured this classic image at Arecibo, Puerto Rico, in January, 1942. It helps explain why the woodie wagon "Publicos" (pages 126–127) of Puerto Rico were literally "loved to death."

Shop men at Merlin Motors, the Ford dealer in Camden, New Jersey, service a new '41 Ford Station Wagon for the showroom.

A well-kept '41 Mercury Station Wagon at a dealer's garage in 1947.

Photo courtesy of
Kent Jaquith

An accessory-loaded, nicely-cared-for '41 Mercury *Station Wagon* is pictured waiting for service at a Seattle Lincoln–Mercury dealer. The glossy wood body and fabric top suggests a recent varnishing. Ford advised this be done on a regular basis. Even the wagons' chief designer Bob Gregorie said you had to be careful (in damp areas) or, "you'd grow a crop of mushrooms up in the roof ribs." Because of the general lack of care, the vulnerable wood-bodied wagons typically looked abused after a few years which often resulted in poor resale value.

1937 SEIBERT "ARISTOCRAT" ELEVEN-PASSENGER FORD STATION WAGON

$1,310 Toledo

"An excellent job for airport, hotel and resort service."

1941 SEIBERT ELEVEN-PASSENGER MERCURY STATION WAGON

$1,925 Toledo

"The Mercury Station Wagon is a beautiful job, especially adapted for Schools, Resorts, Airports, Country Estates and Hotels."

Photos courtesy of the Bob Jones collection

THE SHOP OF SEIBERT

Woodies weren't that common, but to see one with more doors was a real head-turner! Maker of most six-door station wagons was The Shop of Seibert in Toledo, Ohio, who sold them through Ford dealers. Seibert was the nation's largest producer of custom busses and ambulances and in 1935 began extending the frames of regular passenger Ford V-8s by three-feet and adding two extra doors and more seats. These wagons found popularity mostly among stage companies out west who needed something smaller than a bus on long hauls in sparse areas. In 1937 they offered the *"Aristocrat"* – a stunningly stretched station wagon for visitors to places like Montana's Glacier National Park.

Seibert offered these Ford-only wagons every model year until at least 1949 and recommended low gear ratio axles and heavy-duty tires. Stretched to 20 feet, the big '41 Mercury two-tonner pictured was comfortable touring at its best, with three full seats and two buckets in genuine cowhide.

HAY & HARDING
LIMITED
ES, VANS, TRUCK BODIES

Crafty Canadians made this custom wagon out of a brand-new '41 Ford Pickup.

Photos courtesy of the Glenbow Museum, Calgary

A mortuary in Calgary, Alberta, Canada, thought a Ford station wagon would make a nice funeral car, but they needed something with a tad longer load space. So they called on the pioneer Hay & Harding Body company of that city to build them something special. What re-sulted was this one-of-a-kind wood-bodied casket hauler, skilfully crafted from a new '41 Ford Pickup. Note the angle of the windshield, the front-end styling, and the full-steel running boards. Canadians always liked their Fords a bit different from their U.S. cousins, regardless of the cost.

WAR WAGONS
1940-44

"For desert reconnaissance only captured English (Ford) trucks are to be employed. German trucks stick in the sand." FIELD MARSHAL ERWIN ROMMEL, 1941

Since the U.S was neutral in World War II before Pearl Harbor, Ford U.S. didn't officially supply military vehicles to any of the combatants. Unofficially, it supplied a lot of them from its subsidiary plants around the world — primarily the one across the river from Detroit at Windsor, Ontario, Canada.

The Canadians had entered the war against Germany in September 1939, in support of their Commonwealth ally England. In 1940, Canada was providing men, food, and materiel for the British defense, including 5,000 military vehicles. Most of these were staff cars and "Special" Army trucks but they also included 416 Iron Mountain-bodied Ford station wagons for use of Canadian and British forces.

In February, 1941, Hitler sent General Erwin Rommel to the Libyan desert to reinforce Mussolini's collapsing Italian army. There, the British 8th Army would struggle against Rommel's Afrika Korps for nearly two years.

The British fight in North Africa would require a massive supply of combat vehicles, including a rush order to Ford Canada in Windsor for a thousand 1941 Ford station wagons to be converted for desert fighting. The bodies were from Ford, Iron Mountain in Michigan. The finished vehicles were to be crated wheels off, and shipped around the Cape of Good Hope and up the Red Sea to the British Army on the Nile.

The contract for the wagons, dated March 1, 1941, was handled by the Canadian Department of Munitions and Supply in Ottawa. It specified how the wagons were to be modified and equipped at an agreed price of $1,109.70 each. Deliveries were to begin in April, 1941, and be completed by July.

In total, it was the largest single military order for Ford station wagons in World War II.

The wagons were mostly for the use of the SAS, an elite British commando unit trained for hit–and-run fighting and scouting behind enemy lines. Specifications included dowelled wood joints at key points, desert-colored paint inside and out, gun racks and map tables, night-running black out lights, fast Mercury V-8 engines equipped to run cooler, longitudinal rear springs to handle rolling terrain, a low-geared rear axle borrowed from the Ford One-Tonner truck, and 9.00x13 balloon "flotation" tires for speeding across the burning sands.

On December 7, 1941, Japan attacked Pearl Harbor resulting in a declaration of war by the U.S. By February 1942, all production of the nation's civilian passenger cars was ordered stopped and the plants turned to the war effort. This meant, among other things, that the Ford plant at Iron Mountain, Michigan would be shut down, and the building of wood station wagon bodies would be stopped for the duration of the war.

The plant's manager, Walter Nelson, was told by headquarters in Dearborn that he would have to find a war job to keep the plant open. Nelson quickly searched out a large military project that required specialized wood skills. In April, 1942, he won the bid to produce 1,000 CG-4 transport gliders for the U.S. Army Air Corps.

The plant reopened and retooled to build the complex plywood wings for the gliders. The fuselage itself was all metal. Its construction was subcontracted then brought in for wing-fit. After assembly, the completed unit was knocked-down, crated, and shipped to the war front.

The first Ford glider was completed and test-flown in December 1942. Iron Mountain would go on to build 80 percent of all the U.S. gliders produced in World War II.

Meanwhile, the plant received more war jobs to keep the men working. These included supplying wood flooring, tables, and shelving for military offices and barracks, making wood parts for jeeps and trucks, and furnishing strategic by-products like ethyl alcohol.

In November 1944, with the end of conflict in sight, the glider contract was cancelled and Walter Nelson and his men started thinking again about what they did best— building those classy wood station wagon bodies out of a raw log. ◆

Photos and research courtesy of Sandy Notarianni, Historical Consultant, Public Affairs, Ford Motor Company of Canada Limited.

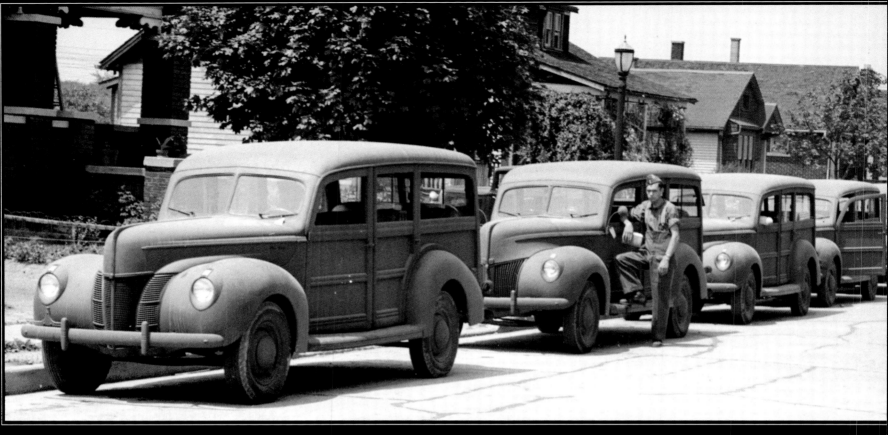

Led by a Deluxe model, a string of mostly 1940 Ford Standard station wagons in war paint line up for orders outside the Ford-Canada plant in Windsor, Ontario.

1940 Canadian Ford military Staff Wagon

1944 FORD ARMY WAGON

There were station wagons built by Ford [d]uring WWII! On Army orders, Ford sent new [4]4 military 2-door sedans to Schult Trailer [Co.] in Middlebury, Indiana, to be converted [in]to "Auxiliary Ambulance and Carryall" units [fo]r the Normandy invasion. Schult, the [ol]dest U.S. trailer house maker, also did [ot]her military work. Just one of these wag[o]ns are known to survive — SW63 (*Station Wagon 63*), built in May, 1944, by the data [pl]ate. It was bought off a truck headed for [th]e scrap yard and restored by Al Finseth [of] Wisconsin, who found a WWII bullet in [th]e body.

Right, and below: The Schult Army wagon [ha]d a fabric roof with steam–bent oak top [b]ows, oak body framing, and masonite [p]anelling. Inside, facing side seats flipped [d]own for troops, or up for ambulance use. [Fli]p-down step plates up a side body post [le]d to the spare in the roof rack. Bridging [u]nderneath supported the extra 24-inch [re]ar body length.

For a hurry-up war job, Schult showed some artistry in the Ford wagon's rear body design. The bumper was cut for a foldaway step.

Built for combat, not looks, the 1944 Ford Army wagon bodies were patched on to

The 29 millionth Ford – a 1941 Super Deluxe Station Wagon – came off the assembly line in Dearborn, Michigan, April 29, 1941. It was presented to the local Red Cross Motor Corps by Ford Company president Edsel Ford. A pretty volunteer driver is pictured with the milestone car which featured wavy-grained Gumwood panelling.

Ready for any emergency, a fleet of 1940-42 Ford ambulances are pictured at a San Francisco Red Cross garage shortly after the attack on Pearl Harbor.

Left: Ford-Canada built the first pro-duction Ford station wagons with sun roofs! A neatly-installed "roof hatch" was cut into some 1941-42 military wagons they modified so Army commandos had

Unfinished 1942 Ford-Mercury station wagon body panels at the closed Iron Mountain plant June 13, 1942.

Finished 1942 station wagon doors won't be hung until war's end after the Ford Iron Mountain plant stopped everything to build military gliders.

WORLD WAR II EQUIPMENT PRODUCED BY FORD

When the U.S. entered World War II in 1942, Ford's Iron Mountain plant was turned from making station wagons to building 4,291 wood-winged military gliders to land troops and equipment. Two glider types were built: a 15-passenger model, and one that held 42. The larger of the two is pictured on the runway of the famed Ford Willow Run bomber plant in a "family portrait" of all the military planes and equipment produced by Ford in World War II. Besides gliders, that included B-24 Liberator bombers, aircraft and tank engines, jeeps, military trucks, tanks and tank destroyers, amphibians, armored cars, universal carriers, staff cars and tractors. Iron Mountain also produced wood parts for jeeps and trucks.

Eugene T. "Bob" Gregorie 1908–2002

"There were no schools on car design in those days like you have now. You had architects and boat designers like Gregorie. They had to work with their own instincts, unlike designers today who were taught how to get the lines flowing." ROSS COUSINS

STYLING THE WOODIES

Tucker Madawick says that the craftsmanship found in Ford woodies really had to be admired and that they always commanded attention whether they were at rest or moving. "They were like early Chris Craft or Gar Wood speedboats with wheels and were usually associated with top vacation resorts like Pinehurst, Pebble Beach, or Hilton Head. If you liked horses, played golf, or sailed, these were your cars!"

That's how he remembers them back in their heyday. Yet within the Ford Design Department, where he had a hand in styling them from 1939 to 1942, how sketches of the wood-bodied station wagons left his hands to become such beauties is mostly a mystery. Nobody seemed to know much about them except the boss, chief stylist Bob Gregorie. "In all my years with Gregorie," Madawick recalls. "the wagons were untouchable. They were treated like India's Sacred Cow! "

He thinks the reason for this was that the wood bodies for these models were so special that they were handled as "outside jobs" — meaning at Iron Mountain — instead of the big Rouge plant in Dearborn where the regular steel car bodies were built.

Gregorie himself didn't think there was much his department had to do in designing a station wagon.

In his last interview ever, given for this book shortly before his death December 1, 2002, at the age of 94, the still quick-minded legendary Ford chief designer said designing a station wagon body really wasn't much different from making a nice piece of furniture.

"As a matter of fact," he said, " I didn't spend much time with the station wagons. The requirements were all pretty much the same. There wasn't much design work to do, so there was never a (design) breakthrough so to speak. It was completely loose. There was no tooling involved, compared to a production steel automobile. It was basically a carpenter's job. So you had all kinds of leeway. We didn't make a clay model. The whole thing was primarily from a drawing."

A lot of these drawings were made by Ross Cousins, who got a job in Ford Design in 1938 as an illustrator and worked on the boards with Madawick. He said his assignments, "usually started with Gregorie saying to me, 'I'd like you to make up some sketches of this in a real life situation.'

He, himself, was a pretty good sketcher. He would sketch a lot in front of Edsel. And he would do the same for me."

After Edsel Ford approved a station wagon design, the sketch would then go to Murray Corporation's design department which did the body engineering and plans for all such work since 1929. They also continued to furnish the special sheet metal needed to build the wagon bodies.

"It was up to (Murray) where to put the joints," said Gregorie, "unless we wanted to feature certain areas. But generally it didn't make much difference where you put the joints. Just so that it had good proportions and there was a wood pattern effect.

"We would furnish Murray the drawings for the sheet metal, and the stampings would be sent up there (to Iron Mountain) who did the layout so the wood would fit the sheet metal like the cowl and floorpan and adjoining metal parts. Then the finished body was sent (to the assembly plants) complete for installing."

In every instance since 1929, Edsel made the important decisions on station wagons, and all Ford styling, up to his death in 1943. An example of this are some 1941 Ford and Mercury station wagon design notations in the files of the Henry Ford Museum Research Center. They reveal how he rejected and approved until he had just the right look and feel of interior materials, from trim and instrument panels, to the grain pattern of leather seats.

"We would follow the range of Ford colors," said Gregorie, about how body paint selections were made. "The popular colors for the wagons were tan and ivory tones. In fact, one time I had them paint the body metal to match the maple wood color. It looked very nice. Seats were what we called art (artificial) leather. It looked good and smelled good and gave a nice effect. It held up surprisingly well."

Gregorie said sales of the wagons, however, "were never that good. There wasn't a lot of interest in them. I had several of them. They were surprisingly durable if you sanded them down every couple of years and varnished them. They held up fine. It's surprising the way they turned out. They were under a thousand dollars complete. Now, they're $70,000!"

So creating a Ford station wagon was just a happy accident. And, Bob Gregorie would live to see them become some of the most valued American cars of all time! ◆

To Tuck. No "2" Sout. Bob Gregorie

Station wagons, like all Ford models, were designed behind the tall doors of this building in Dearborn, Michigan.

"It was a wonderful building to work in, designed by Albert Kahn. It was built of reinforced concrete and steel with lots of glass windows for light and even without air conditioning was very cool in the summer. It had beautiful parquet wood floors that a staff of people kept polished." TUCKER MADAWICK

Photos courtesy of Tucker Madawick

Tucker Madawick is pictured in 1939 with his '35 Ford Phaeton outside the Ford Engineering building where he worked in Design. Bob Gregorie's Continental Cabriolet, which was Edsel Ford's second prototype of this great classic, is parked at the doors. Gift of the car was typical of Edsel who rewarded the men who helped him develop a new design, as he had in giving C.W. Avery the second station wagon in 1928.

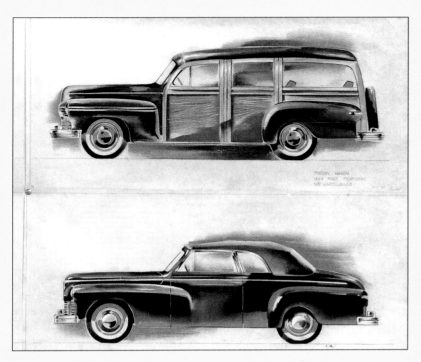

Proposed 1943 Ford cars drawn by Madawick

Tucker Madawick (born 1917) was a Ford design illustrator from 1939-42, then worked on the Ford B-24 bomber project at Willow Run. Later, he was on the '48 Tucker automobile design team, designed Studebakers, and became a VP of design for RCA. Forever youthful, and a classic car collector, among his hands-on restorations has been an original '48 Ford station wagon.

Tucker Madawick draws a Mercury at the Ford Exhibit at the 1939 New York World Fair. Fellow illustrator Ross Cousins etched the panel so the lines could be chalked, erased, and chalked again to please the crowd.

A Ford body engineer works with a design sketch of a 1946 Ford Sportsman to correct problems with the wood construction. Several running changes had to be made to strengthen joints and allow for better water runoff. The photo was taken June 5, 1946.

Right: Influenced by his well-known automotive illustrator father, Ross Cousins (born 1916) was hired by Bob Gregorie in 1938 as Ford's first "design illustrator" to help the advertising companies with their new model ads. He left in 1946 to embark on a remarkable freelance career that included illustrating for Cadillac and Lionel Train. "I worked on visual concepts," says Cousins about his work in Ford Design, "of what it would look like all built. When Edsel came in to look at it he would get a feeling of how it would be in real life. The drawings were to put a little life into it."

"... Ross Cousins and I did all the sketching using pastel as the medium. When Gregorie felt he had sufficient drawings they were matted and presented to Edsel Ford for his critique." TUCKER MADAWICK

"Tuck was a real talent with a nice breezy, quick style and flair." ROSS COUSINS

Ross Cousins, sketching on his new '46 Ford

Ross Cousins sketched this proposed post-war Ford station wagon in a seaside setting in 1944. The Bob Gregorie design evolved into the '49 Mercury.

Ford's out Front

WITH A FAMILY AFFAIR!

Do you know why more people have picked Ford station wagons than any other make? Here's one reason: Ford pioneered the station wagon . . . introduced this smart utility model to an appreciative public. Yes, Ford has produced more cars of this body type than all other makers put together.

Today Ford Continues
to build its own station wagon bodies at Iron Mountain, Michigan . . . selects the finest native hardwoods for them . . . fashions them with real cabinetmaker craftsmanship. "It's the best looking, longest lasting

A trainload of logs arrive at the sawmill.

A sawman makes the first cut into a green hardwood maple log. The rough-cut planks went from here to the dry-kiln. Henry Ford insisted that nothing was wasted. Every wood scrap went to the plant's huge chemical distilleries to be made into useful by-products, like the ethyl alcohol needed to make the station wagon artificial leather seats and tops.

A log destined for wagon body wood moves through a band saw.

Left: An operator gang loads glued-up finger-joint blanks into a press that will bond then under pressure at the right angle to be curve-shaped.

Below: Chips fly as door frame sections are shaped from blocks of maple or birch. The parts will go through a battery of shapers before they are ready for assembly.

Bonding the famous Ford station wagon finger joints

Putting the curve in a front door pillar

1946 wagon wood assembly began with about 300 men building the door and body panels.

Seasoned Iron Mountain assemblers match grains from select stocks of shaped, mortised and tenoned maple or birch to build a rear door frame in a layout jig. The door and body frames were built by painting the raw wood joints with special moisture and mold-resistant resin glue, then joining them together and applying clamping pressure until they were bonded.

Left: Assembled rear quarter panels move on overhead conveyors towards the body bucks.

Below: Primed cowls, rear fenders, tailgate hinges and other parts were conveyed through the dryer tunnels that were equipped with hundreds of gold-plated heat lamps. The special wagon fenders were shipped inside the bodies to be finish-painted at the assembly plants.

Metal parts were primed and dried, then sent to the body-build bucks.

Photos courtesy of the Brad and Barbara Smith collection

Building a Ford wagon door required furniture-quality craftsmanship. Here, the rear door window mechanism has been installed in the frame with glass and trim. Then the fine, pre-cut mahogany or gum plywood panels were fit in place with finishing screws and flat washers.

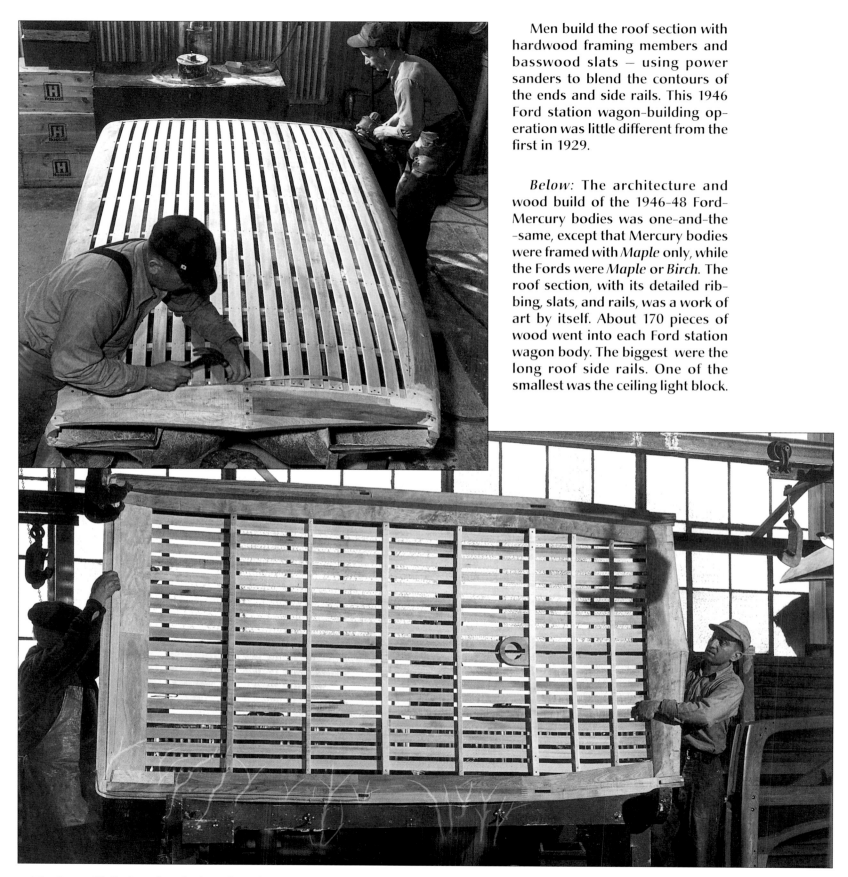

Men build the roof section with hardwood framing members and basswood slats – using power sanders to blend the contours of the ends and side rails. This 1946 Ford station wagon–building operation was little different from the first in 1929.

Below: The architecture and wood build of the 1946-48 Ford-Mercury bodies was one-and-the-same, except that Mercury bodies were framed with *Maple* only, while the Fords were *Maple* or *Birch*. The roof section, with its detailed ribbing, slats, and rails, was a work of art by itself. About 170 pieces of wood went into each Ford station wagon body. The biggest were the long roof side rails. One of the smallest was the ceiling light block.

The beautifully handcrafted roof section of the 1946-48 Ford and Mercury station wagons

The assembled wood panels and steel floor were joined and aligned in a special body-buck.

The wagon body took shape as the pre-painted steel floorpan, primed cowl and windshield assembly, and door pillars, were laid down on the framing fixture or "body buck." The sides and roof were moved on and the "panellers" began bolting on metal attaching brackets at key points. Then, in one of the most critical steps, the doors were hung and adjusted so they had perfect spacing, swung freely, and didn't bind. With everything in proper alignment, the bodies moved on to the main line for finishing.

Aligned with a myriad of air clamps and screw jack devices, a fully assembled body shell is ready to be fitted with wood skids and dolly wheels. It will then be moved down the line on channel tracks to the next operation.

A wheel housing is arc-welded into place with the floorpan. Working with steel gave Iron Mountain the skills it would soon need to build the wood-panelled all-metal 1949 bodies.

Hand-built and hand-sanded. Iron Mountain men who have worked the wood of thousands of station wagons over the years, block sand 1946 side panels with fine-grade paper in preparation for varnish.

At final count, 50,287 hand-finished 1946-48 model station wagon bodies were turned out by Iron Mountain.

Rolled slowly down the 500 foot main line in stops and starts, the fully-assembled station wagon bodies were given a hand-sanding with fine grit paper. Then the body was washed inside and out with naptha gas, a petroleum-based cleaner, and inspected with a light for blemishes. Bodies needing fixing were rolled to the side for repairs.

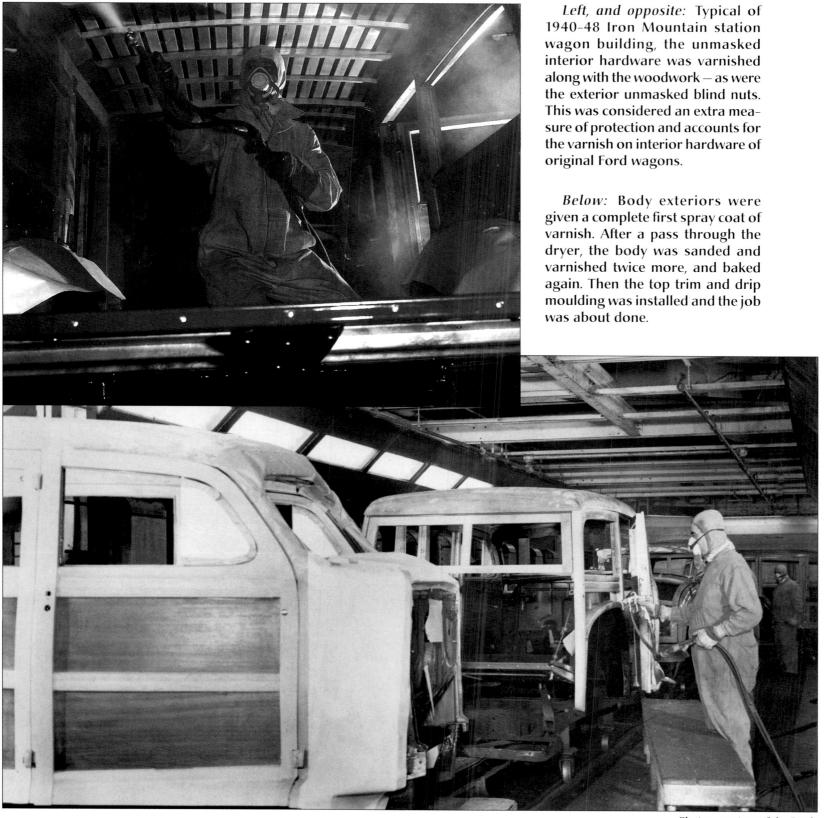

Left, and opposite: Typical of 1940-48 Iron Mountain station wagon building, the unmasked interior hardware was varnished along with the woodwork — as were the exterior unmasked blind nuts. This was considered an extra measure of protection and accounts for the varnish on interior hardware of original Ford wagons.

Below: Body exteriors were given a complete first spray coat of varnish. After a pass through the dryer, the body was sanded and varnished twice more, and baked again. Then the top trim and drip moulding was installed and the job was about done.

Metal parts except blindnuts masked, 1946 station wagon and sportsman (beyond) bodies get a first coat of exterior varnish. The bodies were masked to receive, according to Ford, "three coats of varnish to bring out the natural wood grain and produce a rich lustre."

Photos courtesy of the Brad and Barbara Smith collection

Every surface of the interior was given a coat of varnish before parts like dome light and door handles were installed. Most years the wagon floors were painted black, sometimes brown, sometimes a combination of both. In some instances the bottom was left red primer. All, seemingly at the whim of the painter. The rear interior wheel housings were usually specified bracket-color brown.

A finished 1946 body in primer, fully trimmed with glass, seats, top and wiring, awaits loading in a boxcar for shipment to an assembly plant.

Photos courtesy of the Brad and Barbara Smith collection

Right: After a high-pressure shower to check for leaks, the wagon bodies were loaded eight or ten to a boxcar for shipment to the distant assembly plants. Hydraulic dollies were used to lift the top units which were secured to fixed steel frames. In general, all Iron Mountain wagon bodies from the first 1940 models were shipped out in prime coat. They would get body color at their destination assembly plant where they would be matched to dealer orders and chassis. (Note that the one being loaded also needs windshield glass.) Here also were installed the Ford or Mercury upholstery trim and seats.

Ford station wagon bodies are basically the same 1946-48. Spare cover and lock came standard.

"The hickory and hardwood braces, panels and trim of your new station wagon have been carefully rubbed and varnished to a glowing rich beauty... All woods absorb a certain amount of extra moisture if left in the open, and therefore your station wagon should be kept in your garage when not in use... to protect the appearance and durability of its hardwood body." YOUR NEW STATION WAGON, *1947 GLOVE COMPARTMENT CARD*

1946–48 FORD–MERCURY STATION WAGONS

Specifications in general

CHASSIS & EQUIPMENT – Fords have 114-inch wheelbase. 100 h.p. V-8, or 90 h.p. Six engine. Mercurys have 118-inch wheelbase. 100 h.p. V-8 engine. Standard equipment includes 6.00x16 6-ply tires for Fords, and 6.50x15 6-ply tires for Mercurys, both with spare tire covers and locks.

BODY

1946 Ford has *Maple* or *Birch* frame (also some *Hickory* as specified 1947-48). Mercury has *Maple* frame. Ford has *Mahogany* or *Gumwood* panels. Mercury has *Mahogany* or *Birch* panels *Basswood* roof slats. Top fabric color is M2600-G *Brown* artificial leather.

INTERIOR

1946 Ford seats are *Golden Tan* genuine leather trimmed in *Tan* vinyl (or all vinyl). Seats in 1947-48 Fords are *Tan* vinyl. 1946 Mercury seats are *Tan, Red,* or *Gray genuine leather*. 1947-48 Mercury seats are *Tan,* or *Red genuine leather.* 1946 Ford instrument panel is *Maplewood Grain* or *Coppersand Metallic* (also *Brown Metallic*). 1947-48 Ford instrument panel is *Maplewood Grain*. 1946-48 Mercury instrument panel is *Mahogany wood-grain*. 1946-48 Ford-Mercury floor mats are black rubber.

Source:
1946-48 Ford Passenger Car Prices & Options
1944-52 Ford Body Parts Catalog
1946-47 Ford Passenger Car Sales Handbook
1946-48 Mercury sales letters

1947 Ford Super Deluxe Station Wagon

When you look inside the Mercury Station Wagon, spacious comfort greets the eye! Smartly upholstered in soft, durable, genuine leather, there's plenty of seat, head, leg and shoulder room for eight grown-ups.

Easy removal of the center and rear seats quickly converts the Mercury Station Wagon into an efficient utility hauling vehicle. Tail gate may be lowered to a horizontal position to increase loading length.

A black-draped portrait of Henry Ford with a "1947" Mercury Station Wagon.

"Buyers of the new Ford, Mercury, and Lincoln passenger cars are receiving 1947 titles to their vehicle although the cars are still the same models as produced in 1946. Ford is using this procedure to protect buyers on valuations in the future when their cars are either sold or traded on new models. The company is planning face-lifted versions to be introduced possibly in late March." *DETROIT FREE PRESS, MARCH 2, 1947*

'47 WOODIES WITH '46 FEATURES

Pictured above, a Detroit dealer pays tribute to Henry Ford with a representative '47 Mercury *Station Wagon* shortly after the famous automaker's death on April 7, 1947. A '47 Mercury with '46 styling? Yes. In one of those peculiarities that needs explaining, the 1947 model cars were late in delivery, which caused a dealer inventory build-up of 1946 models well into spring. Understandably, they were now harder to sell. A quick title change made them '47s, at a higher price. The dealers loved it. Car-starved buyers didn't seem to mind because they now had a new '47 model with all the benefits. Thus, several thousand '46 Ford and Mercury-styled station wagons went on the road as '47s.

A 1946 Chevrolet Fleetmaster station wagon makes a popular photo stop at the giant "Tunnel Tree" in California's Sequoia National Park. Hard as they tried, no U.S. auto company came close to Ford's dominance of the wood-bodied station wagon market.

THE COMPETITION

There were other wood-bodied station wagons out on the road besides the Fords described in this book. But from the beginning, the famous Fords owned the market, taking seventy percent of all sales of these types in 1946. Besides *Chevrolet,* other wood-bodied wagon sellers in the post-war era included *Oldsmobile, Pontiac, Buick, Plymouth, Willys,* and *Packard.* Like Ford's *Sportsman Convertible,* Chrysler catered to swank appeal with its own wood-decked *Town and Country Convertible,* and *Town and Country Sedan.* The 1953 Buicks are considered the last true "woodie" station wagons.

1947-48 MERCURY STATION WAGON Model 79
1947 production – 3,558
1948 production – 1,889

1947, $1,849 Detroit
1948, $2,075 Detroit

Body by Ford, Iron Mountain

Right: The photographer's lens bends the front-end of a new '47 Mercury *Station Wagon* waiting to be serviced at a Lincoln–Mercury dealer. Quick identification of the 1946-48 Mercurys is the hood trim running along the belt-line from the door. The '47-48 strip is shorter. Its grille is also full chrome.

Introduced to put some sizzle in post-World War II sales, the sexy maple and mahogany '46 Ford Sportsman convertible is one of the most famous woodies of all time.

1946 FORD SUPER DELUXE SPORTSMAN CONVERTIBLE COUPE *Model 69A-71B* $1,980 Detroit   *Body by Ford, Iron Mountain*
Production – 1,209

NEW SPORTSMAN

The *Sportsman* was conceived by Ford stylists to fill the need for a body style between the station wagon and the convertible. Wood portions of the body consist of selected hardwoods and mahogany panels with durable varnish which adds depth and richness to the grain of the natural wood. The *Sportsman* is built only in the *Super Deluxe* model with V-8 engine. *FORD MODELS AND EQUIPMENT* _____

Actress Ella Raines in Hollywood with the first Ford Sportsman Convertible.

To stir up publicity about the new *Sportsman* "station wagon convertible," Ford delivered the first one built to film actress Ella Raines in Hollywood, California, Christmas Day, 1945. The star of *"White Tie and Tails"* is pictured on a Universal Studios lot shortly before having her initials monogrammed on the doors. A real head-turner wherever it appeared during an intense publicity campaign, it would be Admiral Halsey's car as Grand Marshall to lead the famous parade in the 1946 Pasadena Tournament of Roses.

Opposite: Women persuading their husbands to buy was the primary aim of Ford's 1946 *Sportsman* marketing. One of the new wood-panelled beauties beckons suggestively from ladies apparel in a fashionable department store.

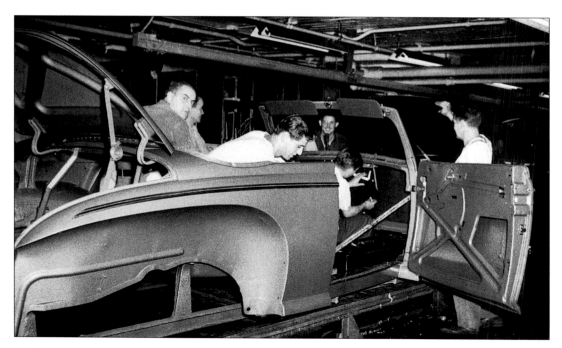

The Sportsman was built from a regular production Ford convertible body.

A completed 1946 Ford Sportsman body at Iron Mountain, ready for trim.

Top: Ford's chief stylist Bob Gregorie said designing the *Sportsman* was easy. He just took the metal skins off the convertible doors, deck lid, and rear quarters and worked on some wood.

Right: The *Sportsman* bodies were customized at about one for every twenty-five station wagon units built on the parallel main line at the Iron Mountain plant. Regular convertible panel skins were replaced with modified ones. Then the bodies were primed, rolled back to the line to have wood fitted, sent to be varnished, and back again for trim.

Iron Mountain workers test the top mechanism and put finishing touches on one of the very low production 1946 Mercury Sportsman bodies.

1946 MERCURY SPORTSMAN Model 71
Production – 205

$2,250 Detroit

Body by Ford, Iron Mountain

The 1946 Mercury *Sportsman* had such great promise, but nice as it was, it just never took off in the marketplace. At $270 less, buyers could see a better value in the equally beautiful Ford version of the glossy wood-bodied convertible. So, on September 9, 1946 it was discon-tinued after a run of just five months. It would go down in automotive history as one of the rarest production Ford convertibles ever made. Of the survivors, it is said that only one in original factory condition still exists — last reported in the hands of an Indiana collector.

Above and right: A good way to a pretty girl's heart was a new '46 Mercury *Sportsman Convertible!*

1947-48 FORD SUPER DELUXE SPORTSMAN CONVERTIBLE COUPE* Model 79A-71b   *$2,150 Detroit   Body by Ford, Iron Mountain
1947 production — 2,250
1948 production — 28

Photos courtesy of the Brad
and Barbara Smith collection

A classy Sportsman *steals the show at the Ford exhibit at the 1947 Mid-America Fair in Cleveland, Ohio.*

Glamorous and crowd pleasing as it was, the Ford *Sportsman* convertible was still not an easy sale in the summer of 1947. Not even when the price was dropped a hundred dollars. Buyers were skittish about the upkeep and rumors, which proved to be true, that the earlier '46 models were prone to mildew, that wood joints came apart, and that the rear deck lid didn't fit. But for Ford dealers, the new improved *Sportsman* was good for bringing in upscale customers — and just the price you had to pay for the best looking car in the neighborhood.

Sportsman convertibles were assembled with the new '47 features (above and opposite) beginning April 1, 1947. Compared to the regular Ford convertible seats which were combination vinyl and cord cloth, the *Sportsman* seats were richly tailored with full *genuine leather* facings in a choice of *Tan* or *Red* with french stitching. Carpet floor mat inserts were a nice touch but had to be protected from muddy foot prints. Each '47 *Sportsman* glove compartment came with a handy copy of *"Ford and Mercury Station Wagon and Sportsman Convertible Wood Body Preservation and Repair."*

A new Ford Super Deluxe Sportsman Convertible Coupe *April 24, 1947*

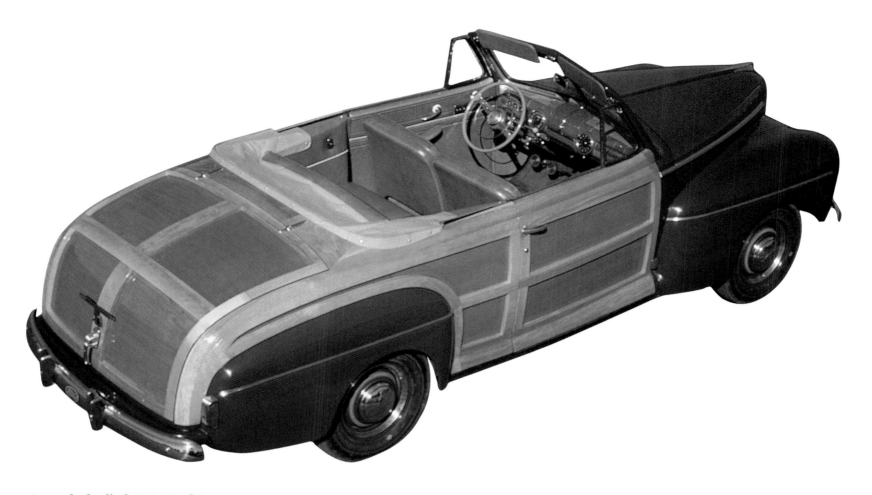

An early-bodied 1946 Ford Sportsman

1946-48 FORD-MERCURY SPORTSMAN
Specifications in general

CHASSIS & EQUIPMENT – Ford has 114-inch wheelbase. 100 h.p. V-8. Mercury has 118-inch wheelbase. 100 h.p. V-8. Standard equipment includes top boot and automatic windows. Ford has 6.00x16 tires. Mercury has 6.50x15 tires.

BODY
Hard *maple* frame
Mahogany plywood panels

INTERIOR AND TOP

1946 Ford seats facings are *Golden Tan, Red,* or *Blue Gray genuine leather.* 1947-48 Ford seats facings are *Golden Tan,* or *Red genuine leather,* or *Tan* or *Red genuine leather* with pebble grain finish. Balance of seats are vinyl

plastic leather. The 1946-48 Ford instrument panel is *Maplewood Grain.* The 1946 Mercury instrument panel is *Mahogany-grain.* Canvas top material is optional *Black* or *Drab Tan.* Boot to match top color. Red piping on the '46 top. Piping to match top on '47-48.

1946 FORD-MERCURY BODY METAL COLORS

Light Moonstone Gray, Navy Blue, Botsford Blue Green, Modern Blue, Dynamic Maroon, Greenfield Green, Dark Slate Gray Metallic, Silver Sand Metallic, Willow Green, Black.

1947-48 FORD BODY METAL COLORS

Medium Luster Black, Rotunda Gray, Barcelona Blue, Monsoon Maroon, Glade Green, Feather Gray, Parrott Green Metallic, Tucson Tan, Taffy Tan, (plus *Strata Blue* and *Shoal Gray* for '48 models).

Pictured above and top right, part of a series, are the only known factory color photos of a Ford *Sportsman.* While very early production models they provide a wealth of information for restorers. Note the buttons on the side panels for the hydraulic windows.

Iron Mountain's execution of the *Sportsman* was a masterpiece of wood shaped, bent, and finger-jointed to perfection. A lesson learned on the early bodies, like the one above, was that the rear deck cross piece was too high and trapped water. On '47 models, it was beveled and moved lower near the license plate (like the car on the left) so water ran off. The *Sportsman* rear fenders and taillights were borrowed from the '41 Ford *Sedan Delivery*.

A Ford Sportsman in the showroom of Stuart Wilson Ford in Dearborn, Michigan, September 16, 1947

Ford had an entire Hollywood publicity department devoted to getting the 1946-48 models in the movies. These stills are from MGM's "*The Sun Come Up*," starring Jeanette McDonald, Lassie, and a pretty '47 *Sportsman*.

Opposite: A wagon load of cowgirls at the San Francisco introduction of the sensational new '49 Ford models.

1949-51

The Iron Mountain plant with its train of arriving logs makes an appropriate backdrop March 22, 1948, for 1949 Ford Station Wagon number one. The beautiful all-new two-doors with laminated panels over steel bodies would make their public debut seven weeks later.

CLASSY LAST WOODIES
1949-51

The outlook for selling station wagons, going into the unprecedented post-WWII boom seemed boundless. American families had discovered that for the money, sporty appeal, and all-round usefulness, this was the ideal car.

It looked good in the driveway. It was great for hauling kids, dogs, garden tools and groceries. And nothing was better for towing a boat and bringing along everything from the whole family – to fishing tackle, cots, lanterns, and tents on those weekend camping trips.

GM and Chrysler saw the sudden interest in family wagons and began tooling up new all-steel models. It was late 1947. Ford, too, had a steel wagon body underway. Its studies had found that an all-steel station wagon body would cost about $100 less per unit to build than one from wood, save on upkeep, and with less deterioration, would have a higher resale value. But their marketing surveys also showed that ninety percent of potential Ford station wagon buyers would rather have one with the traditional sporty wood look.

Here, Ford had a distinct selling advantage. With its big Iron Mountain plant available to produce the wood customers expected, it was decided to bring out the new all-steel bodied '49 Ford and Mercury 2-door station wagons with hand-crafted genuine wood panels.

The problem was that choice framing maple and birch in the volumes needed had become scarce. The new wagons had shapely lines, which presented another dilemma. Huge amounts of valuable hardwood would be wasted in cutting the body curves from straight stock.

Iron Mountain plant manager Walter Nelson came up with the solution. From building WWII gliders he was familiar with the aircraft industry's use of lightweight lamination where sandwiches of thin wood strips were glued, then bent

All photos in this chapter courtesy of Ford Motor Company, except where noted.

and heat bonded in a mold to produce amazingly strong and graceful lightweight shapes.

Adapting this idea to the new Ford and Mercury station wagons, cheaper wood strips such as elm could be used on the inside, with the prettier maple on the outer faces. The technique was tried. The savings were impressive! Lamination used a third less material than solid wood, and in making the station wagon panels, saved as much as sixty percent in man hours! On March, 22, 1948, the first '49 Ford pilot model station wagon with laminated wood (opposite) was built at Iron Mountain.

The steel bodies themselves were welded together at the plant with newly learned skills. "We had to start from scratch," said Nelson, "as we had never done any metal finishing or painting. Those operation were new to us . . . I sent two men to Twin Cities (Ford assembly plant) to watch their metal-finishing operations. With those two men as a nucleus, we built the organization around them."

The beautiful new '49 Ford station wagons made their public debut with the rest of the passenger car line less than three months later, on June 8, 1948. It was with much fanfare at New York City's swank Waldorf Astoria Hotel.

Nearly a year later, after producing exactly 22,114 Ford station wagon bodies, and 6,900 Mercurys (body plant manager Mark Swanson's production report), the workers at Iron Mountain went on a 30-day strike. It started on May 9, 1949, over the age-old gripe of wages and job security. "We were trying to get our costs down," said Nelson. "Every time we made a cost study, it resulted in someone being laid off. Work in the community was scarce, and the people were on edge . . . even then the walkout could have been prevented. The people didn't want to go out, and they were very happy to come back."

Company president Henry Ford II was outraged at the costly loss of production. He had always feared that the union at Iron Mountain would be trouble. Now, after saving 2,000 woodworking jobs, they had walked out on him. He sent vice-president of operations Lewis Crusoe up to Iron Mountain to negotiate.

Barrett McGregor, who grew up there, was the son of an insurance agent not affected by the happenings at Ford. He remembers a story about Crusoe's visit. It was night, and on seeing the plant, he said to his driver, "Can you get me a 30.06? The driver said, 'What for?' So I can shoot out those lights ("Ford" emblazoned on the smokestacks), said Crusoe, so they'll understand how easy this place is to shut down!"

Work commenced again on June 2, 1949. That November 18th, the new 1950 Fords were introduced, followed eleven days later by the Mercurys.

Henry Ford II never forgot the Iron Mountain walk-out or the continued worker agitation there all through 1951 production. The new '52 station wagon bodies were being designed with just a token amount of wood trim. They were going to be built at the Rouge plant in Dearborn.

It made his decision easy. In August, 1951, the entire Iron Mountain property was put up for sale, sending a shockwave through the community which was almost totally dependent on Ford. "The change from wood to steel bodies in the automobile business," explained Ford headquarters," signalled an eventual end to this type operation which currently necessitates shipping almost all the parts for the wagon bodies into Iron Mountain, and then shipping them out again."

The last Iron Mountain Ford station wagon was built on December 5, 1951. The plant was closed and sold to the Kingsford Chemical Company, which advertised to the local townspeople that anyone interested in leftover wagon doors and panels for firewood could help themselves at a dollar a truckload.

It was the end to one of the great legends of Ford Motor Company. ◆

A finished door pillar blank is removed from the bonding press.

Scarcity of quality maple and birch had made the traditional all-wood station wagon body obsolete. So, with the new '49 Fords, aircraft lamination techniques were adapted to make classy wood-saving panels that attached over an all-steel body. Layers of thin plys were bent, molded and bonded under pressure and heat into the graceful, compound curves needed to make the nine different door, quarter panel, window, and tailgate frames. A first for station wagons, Ford molded laminates were actually stronger, more moisture resistant, and had less tendency to warp or split than solid wood.

Cut from a pre-shaped block, raw stock maple veneers are prepared for lamination.

Maple or birch veneer faces on the outside, a resin-glued package of plys for the new
'49 Ford laminated door-frame pillar is inserted into an Iron Mountain bonding press.

This neat wood-panelled '49 Ford was a prototype for a planned 1950 Sportsman
Convertible.

A badged '49 Ford Sportsman Coupe *concept for 1950, loaded with some wild
proposed accessories.*

Ford seriously considered two *Sports-man* models for the 1950–51 line. The wood-panelled bodies were to be built at Iron Mountain, with the required sheet metal stampings from C.W. Avery's Murray Corp. The classy project was dropped when Ford opted to go with the airfoil-panelled new '50 Ford *Crestliner*.

On May 13, 1949, C.W. Avery, the sixty-seven year-old chairman of the board of Murray Corporation of America, died of a heart attack at his farm near Kalamazoo, Michigan. Among the pallbearers at his funeral was the late Edsel Ford's son, Henry Ford II.

During the war years, Avery's Murray company built sub-assemblies and wings for military planes such as the P-47 fighter and the B-29 Super Fortress. Like his inventions of the Ford moving assembly line and glass plants, his methods of mass-production would revolutionize the aircraft industry.

After the war, his company produced a line of metal kitchens and bathrooms to meet the building boom, while continuing to supply metal stampings for the auto industry. It held contracts at Ford to supply Mercury body and frame stampings, as well as sheet metal stampings for the station wagons.

Below: C.W. Avery had a soft-spot for Ford station wagons and owned many. His last was a '48 Mercury. His grandson, Avery Greene, says he often drove prototypes. He is pictured with one of Bob Gregorie's proposals that was the idea for the metal bodied '49 two-door station wagon. It would be typical of Avery to have the car to get a feel for the body stampings needed for the wood panels, as indicated in white.

Clarence W. Avery

C.W. Avery washes a prototype metal-bodied Ford station wagon at his Michigan farm in 1944.

Photos courtesy of the Avery
Greene family archives

The first pilot two-door 1949 Ford station wagon body is pictured in early March, 1948, at Ford Body Engineering in Dearborn. From here it will be shipped to Iron Mountain for fitting the new wood panels to the specially fabricated sides and tailgate. Meanwhile, styists will decide the interior appointments and details like paint colors.

Left: A view of the tailgate stamping showing how the wood panel attached. (Note the pilot Ford convertible body in the background.)

Two-door wagon number one finished "in-the-white" at Dearborn. Once production was approved, Iron Mountain welders would build their own bodies.

At the Iron Mountain wood shops, Ford and Mercury laminated wood frames were built up with mahogany panelling and varnished. In another section of the plant, the steel bodies were built, sanded, primed, painted and sent to the main line. The panels arrived and were fitted on and attached. Then the interior was trimmed. It was the formula for one of Ford's prettiest station wagon series — that lasted with a few modifications from the 1949 through the 1951 models.

Iron Mountain assembly line workers attach finished wood panels to an all-steel 1949 Ford station wagon body.

Attaching the quarter side panel

Photo courtesy of the Brad and Barbara Smith collection

Take a wood body panel off an original Iron Mountain-built Ford or Mercury station wagon and you should find in grease pencil the panel maker's initials and codes including the date it was made. This, and sequentially numbering the bodies (page 242) was for quality control, making each wagon essentially a one-of-a-kind signed copy. Here, assembler Robert Lantz prepares to attach a Ford door panel March 22, 1949.

Robert Lantz carefully bolts the varnished outside wood panel to the painted steel inner door frame of a '49 Ford station wagon body on the final assembly line. More hardware will go on next. Then the interior trim and upholstery, cut and sewn at Iron Mountain, will be installed.

A nicely finished '49 Ford station wagon body arrives at the Iron Mountain loading dock October 7, 1948. It will be shipped out by boxcar to an assembly plant where it will be mated to a chassis, then delivered to a dealer — and ultimately to an eager customer.

Right: The 1949-51 Ford station wagons were assembled on the regular passenger car line but had a modified frame to accommodate the longer bodies and heavier loads. It also had a 60-inch rear axle for wider tread, and 9-leaf rear springs. The Mercurys were only assembled at three U.S. plants: Dearborn, Michigan; Metuchen, New Jersey; and Los Angeles, California.

Experienced hands at the Rouge plant in Dearborn assemble the first 1949 Ford passenger car chassis – a 100 h.p. V-8 – April 10, 1948. The station wagon chassis had a slightly modified frame. Mercurys were built here on a separate line.

1949 FORD CUSTOM DELUXE STATION WAGON Model 98BA-79 (V-8)   *$2,118 Detroit*   *Body by Ford, Iron Mountain*
Production – 31,420   Model 98HA-79 (6-cyl)

Dealers see dollars in the beautiful new '49 Ford Custom Deluxe Station Wagon!

Sporty family station wagons would play a big part in Ford plans for 1949. Los Angeles Ford dealers get their first look at one of the classy new wood-panelled two-doors at the Long Beach assembly plant near Los Angeles shortly before introduction day June 9, 1948.

NEW TWO-DOOR STATION WAGON

Handsome is as handsome does. You'd never think anything so good looking could be so useful! The completely new Ford *Station Wagon* takes eight people anywhere in style and comfort . . . or totes loads up to a half ton with ease! That shiny hardwood body . . . built by the pioneers in station wagons . . . hides a tough steel foundation, for extra safety. The two rear seats can be removed in a matter of minutes. If it's a station wagon you want, it's more than ever a Ford you want! *1949 Ford Advertisement*

NEW '49 MERCURY

The Mercury *Station Wagon* for 1949 is the first full-size, high production vehicle of its type to employ steel construction for all except the wooden body panels. Actually, it is an all-steel shell with wood panelling. Even the top is steel. Safety and durability are more than doubled by the new-type construction. An unusual feature is the use of only two extra-wide doors in place of the usual four-door construction.
LINCOLN-MERCURY NEWS BUREAU, APRIL 20, 1948

Like the Fords, wider doors helped sell the new '49 Mercury station wagons. Having just two was considered safer for children riding in the back.

Right: Veteran Hollywood film star Van Heflin, maybe best remembered for his crusty roles in *"Shane"* and *"Battle Cry,"* is all smiles behind the wheel of his new wagon just picked up at Mercury headquarters in Dearborn.

Below: A Grummon Widgeon float plane parked at Ford Airport in Dearborn makes a sporty backdrop for a classy new Mercury station wagon publicity shot. For traveling types, an extra-cost option for wagons this year was a matched set of mens' or womens' luggage in *Cherrywood* and *Ginger top-grain cowhide.*

Actor Van Heflin with his brand-new '49 Mercury wagon

1949 MERCURY STATION WAGON Model 79B
Production – 8,057

$2,645 Detroit

Body by Ford, Iron Mountain

A '49 Mercury Station Wagon at a country estate. For hauling a bale of hay, pulling a trailer, or taking friends along to a Sunday horse show, its beauty and versatility couldn't be matched.

Still stretching Fords, The Shop of Seibert in Toledo, Ohio, dreamed up this well-proportioned four-door '49 station wagon for hotel limousine service. Fitting in the masterwork extra doors required perfect wood match.

Ford's new '50 Mercury wagon was "top-of-the-line" for suburban America.

Every dog knows when it's time for a ride! A Michigan couple load up their brand-new '50 Mercury *Station Wagon* for a weekend trip. Just the thing for upscale two-car suburbanites it came in a choice of nine enticing colors, including three shades of metallics, and optional *Tan, Red,* or *Green, genuine leather* upholstery.

THE NEW FORD
"Country Squire"
STATION WAGON

So quiet you'll say it whispers whil[e] it works. So good looking you can[']t take your eyes off it. So comfortabl[e] that you travel with passenger-ca[r] ease. So safe it's a "must" for familie[s] with children.

The "Country Squire" is the onl[y] station wagon in its field that offer[s] you choice of famous 100 h.p. V-[8]

There's a *Ford* in your future
with a future built in

MELVILE

sidewall tires and wheel trim rings available at extra cost.

advanced 95 h.p. Six. The ma-
gany-grained outer panels of all-
eel "Lifeguard" Body are trimmed
ith genuine birch or maple.
"Magic-Action" King-Size Brakes
ve 35% easier stopping. And this
pace-happy" Station Wagon still
rries an economy price tag. See
ur Ford Dealer today!

Courtesy of
the Bob Jones
collection

THE MID-'50 MODELS
in war-time

A little understood part of the 1950-51 Ford-Mercury woodie story is why some have steel body panels, and some have wood. Surviving wagons of these years have many other unexplained oddities and differences, compared to ones built at the same time. A review of the situation at the time may provide an explanation.

By early 1950, while sales of the regular Ford passenger cars were the best since 1929, Ford marketers were becoming very concerned about the station wagon business. Buyers were going more for the new all-steel-bodied Chevy's, Pontiacs, and Plymouth Suburbans. Mostly, because they were priced lower than the Fords. But also because steel sides were being pitched by competitors as needing less upkeep than the Ford's wood. The new Suburban had another strong selling point. It had a clever rear seat that folded away nicely into the floor for hauling space.

Salesmen for these makes liked to point out the shortcomings of Ford's wood side panelling, which they said would deteriorate and cause lower resale value. There was no dispute over which of the wagons had more curb appeal. Ford salesmen liked to joke that the stodgy new Plymouth Suburban looked like "a first cousin to a panel truck and stepson of a station wagon." But, nevertheless, its sales had taken off like the proverbial wildfire!

So, Ford made plans to counter all this by bringing out the new, more sophisticated, '51 Ford "Country Squire" and a "modified' Mercury model. They would have the steel panels buyers seemed to want in place of the controversial plywood – and a new "stowaway" center seat that worked better than the Pymouth Suburban's.

Then, in a move to get back in the sales race, Ford decided it was urgent to introduce the new Country Squire, and "modified' Mercury station wagons sooner than later. They hastily moved up introduction of the new models to mid-1950 – five months earlier than originally planned. Full production was started May 29, 1950. Three weeks later the new simulated wood-grained steel-paneled models were introduced to the public with a big advertising blitz.

But the ink was hardly dry on the announcements when on June 24, 1950 – the same week of the introduction – war broke out in Korea, involving the U.S. in what optimists regarded as a "police action" to assist South Korea.

Ford Motor Company took it serious. A month later, it prepared for war production by creating a Defense Production Division. "By early September," wrote Allan Nevins and Frank Ernest Hill, in *FORD: Decline and Rebirth*, "The Detroit press was headlining ominous news. Truman talked of an army of three million men, and on September 8th signed the Defense Production Act which (among other things) . . . set priorities and allocations for critical materials."

The restrictions on materials would soon cover steel, aluminum, copper, nickel, zinc, and rubber. Ford accepted nearly a billion dollars worth of war contracts to produce aircraft engines, bomber wings, trucks and tanks – while still producing a restricted allotment of cars.

Something had to give. Every little bit helped. Ford production managers were asked to cut back wherever they could. So, essentially the new *Country Squire* and Mercury steel panels went into the war effort – and the wood panels were continued.

But not always. Conditions would change according to available materials. Sometimes steel panels were used. Sometimes wood. Adjustments like this happened all through the Korean War until it ended in 1953. Considering the situation, saving on materials may be the primary reason for such changes as going from a full to a half-circle horn ring on the later '51 models – instead of the accepted belief that it was for better vision of the speedometer. A savings here on thousands of cars would be substantial.

Those who remember the new '51 cars saw how quickly the chromework deteriorated. This was because of the restrictions on the materials used – and a real homefront wake-up call that there was a war going on!

According to Iron Mountain body plant manager Mark Swanson's production records, 11,751 regular Custom Deluxe Ford wagon bodies were built between November 1, 1949, and May 28, 1950, when they were discontinued. Production of the new-type '50 Ford Country Squires from May 29, 1950 to October 31, 1950, totalled 11,808 units. In short, the full year production was almost evenly divided between the two types.

Their differences will be always be a good topic of discussion wherever woodie fans meet. ◆

FORD "COUNTRY SQUIRE" STATION WAGON

PONTIAC STANDARD STATION WAGON

The new 1950 Ford Country Squire was rushed into production to counter the hot-selling all-steel Chevrolet, Pontiac and Plymouth Suburban station wagons.

NEW FORD "COUNTRY SQUIRE"

The "Country Squire," a new "double-duty station wagon which can be converted from a comfortable eight-passenger carrier to a one-level-floor cargo in three minutes, has been introduced by Ford Motor Company.

By removing the rear seat of the new Ford station wagon without the use of tools, and folding away the center seat, a level floor surface is created that has a depth of more than nine feet from the back of the driver's seat to the end of the "level-loading" tail gate.

The "Country Squire" features new Mahogany-grained steel side panels, framed with natural Maple or Birch. The new steel side panels add longer life and greater strength to the body.

An all-steel rear deck on which the spare tire is mounted also is a new feature of this model.

Designed as an all-purpose carrier, the new model fulfills the need for a "Sunday calling" station wagon which can be changed quickly to a "Monday hauling" load carrier with minimum effort. FORD NEWS BUREAU, DEARBORN, JUNE 30, 1950

All photos in this chapter courtesy of Ford Motor Company, except where noted.

THE MODIFIED NEW 1950 MERCURY STATION WAGON

A station wagon with an interior designed to permit a flat floor surface from the rear of the driver's seat to the end of the tail gate has been incorporated in the 1950 line of Mercury cars.

This latest version of the 1950 Mercury Station Wagon has acquired additional space for large bulky items by the redesigning of the center seat to a folding type, so the seat back will fold flush with the rear floor has been provided and new support arms permit the tail gate to be lowered and held in a horizontal position.

Mahogany grained steel panels have replaced the exterior plywood panels in this modified 1950 Mercury Station Wagon to increase its ruggedness. A grained all-steel panel is also used on the tail gate. LINCOLN-MERCURY NEWS BUREAU, JUNE 21, 1950 _____

"I want you to know that all of us at Ford Motor Company stand ready to carry out any assignment the government may give us in view of the present situation." HENRY FORD II TELEGRAPH TO PRESIDENT TRUMAN, JULY, 19, 1950

1950 Ford Country Squire *with the new "level-loading floor."*

The 1950 Ford station wagons are a good topic of conversation. In comparing them, the early ones to mid-year have '49-style removable seats and wood body panels. The later ones after mid-year have a lot of differences, including a new center foldaway seat – and paper trans-fer *Mahogany-grained* steel body panels. These were the new *"Country Squires."* The change of panels was another anomaly. While advertised as "steel-grained" on the '50 *Country Squires*, because of the Korean War, many got the earlier *Mahogany* plywood panels.

Above: Load space of the new '50 Ford *Country Squire* was made flat by folding down the center seat and removing the rear seat and replacing it with a filler board. When fully converted, the level deck was nicely finished with heavy-duty ribbed linoleum.

A handier hauler for active families, the new '50 Country Squire *is identified from the outside by the absence of the side glass rear quarter windows.*

In a move to beat the competition, Ford brought out the new *"Country Squire"* with "steel-grained" panelling and center "stowaway" seat on June 30, 1950 — five months earlier than planned. This photo of a family on a picnic at the Dearborn Hills Country Club is the original publicity still used to announce the event. The rowboat was to show how easy it was now to convert the rear to a flat loading space.

The center seat of the mid-year "*modified*" Mercury, like the 1950 Ford *Country Squire*, now folded away into a level load space. The seat back and seat cushion bottom is lined with linoleum to serve as the deck floor. The front and center seat area floor mats are simulated rubber carpeting.

The 1950 "modified" Mercury station wagon center seat folds neatly away into the floor.

Photo courtesy of Dan Brooks

Dealers and the press look over the glamorous new '51 Ford models, including a handsome Country Squire, at a preview at the Masonic Temple in Detroit, November 10, 1950.

1950-51 FORD COUNTRY SQUIRE
Specifications in general

1951 CHASSIS & EQUIPMENT – 114-inch wheelbase. 100 h.p. V-8, or 95 h.p. Six engine. Standard equipment includes 7.10x15 6-ply tires, spare tire and cover.

BODY

Maple or *Birch* framing. *Mahogany-grained* steel or *Mahogany* plywood exterior panels. Body color (1950), or paper-grained steel tailgate (1951).

INTERIOR

Inside door lining is dark-stained plywood. *Golden Tan Vinyl* is used on all 1951 seat cushion tops and fronts of seat backs, with *Dark Brown Vinyl* on lower portion of cushions, tops and sides of seat backs.

1950 seats are two-tone *Tan Vinyl* and artificial leather. Headlining is in *Golden Tan* artificial leather. 1951 has two-tone instrument panel with lower portion in *Dark prima Vera Grain.*

A heavy black rubber mat with simulated carpet inserts is used in driver's compartment. A ribbed black mat is used on floor at center and rear seats. Load compartment floor, interior of tailgate, the back of seatback and bottom of seat cushion of the "stowaway" center seat are tan heavy-duty ribbed linoleum.

1950 BODY METAL COLORS
(same as Custom model page 221)

1951 BODY METAL COLORS

Sheridan Blue, Alpine Blue, Raven Black, Sea Island Green, Silvertone Gray, Mexacalli Maroon Metallic, Hawthorne

The 1951 Ford *Country Squire* had a modified floorpan to accommodate the optional new Fordomatic Drive transmission, which was optional at extra cost. Early '51s had a full-circle steering wheel horn ring. Later rings were half-circle for better instrument view. Some '51s had *Mahogany-grained* "gypsum board" interior panels to match the steel-grained exterior panels. Some had *Mahogany plywood* panels inside and out.

Green Metallic, Greenbriar Metallic, Hawaiian Bronze Metallic, Culver Blue Metallic (Sportsman Green has also been observed on some original wagons)

Source:
1951 Ford Passenger Car Prices and Options
1951 Ford Passenger Car Data Book
1944-52 Ford Body Parts Catalog

1951 MERCURY STATION WAGON Model M79
Production – 3,813

$2,529 Detroit

Body by Ford, Iron Mountain

1949-51 MERCURY STATION WAGONS
Specifications in general

CHASSIS & EQUIPMENT – 118-inch wheelbase. 110 h.p. V-8. Standard equipment includes 7.10x15 6-ply tires, and spare tire and cover.

BODY

Maple and *Mahogany* wood panelling over a steel underbody (1949 and early 50), then *Mahogany-grained* steel panels or *Mahogany* plywood panels.

INTERIOR TRIM

Tan Genuine Leather upholstery is standard in 1949-50 Mercury *Station Wagon* models. *Tan* is available with all body colors. In 1949 models *Red leather* is available with all but *Royal Bronze Blue, Biscay Blue, Berwick Green,* and *Lima Tan. Green leather* is available with *Black, Dakota Gray, Berwick Green,* and *Bermuda Cream* only. In 1950 models *Red leather* is available with all but green body colors. *Green leather* is available in all but *Royal Bronze, Banning Blue,* and *Laguna Blue.* Modified 1950 and 1951 models — *Golden Tan* and *Chestnut Brown all-Vinyl* upholstery available with all body colors. *Two-tone Red all-Vinyl* available in all but green body colors. *Two-tone Green all-Vinyl* available in all but blue and maroon body colors.

1949 BODY METAL COLORS

Black, Alberta Blue, Royal Bronze Maroon Metallic, Dakota Gray, Biscay Blue Metallic, Berwick Green Metallic, Bermuda Cream, Lima Tan Metallic, Tampico Red Metallic.

1950 BODY METAL COLORS

Black, Royal Bronze Maroon, Trojan Gray, Everglade Green, Banning Blue Metallic, Dune Beige, Laguna Blue Metallic, Roanoke Green Metallic, Maywood Green Metallic.

1951 BODY METAL COLORS

Black, Banning Blue Metallic, Everglade Green, Luxor Maroon Metallic, Kerry Blue Metallic, Mission Gray, Coventry Green Gray, Sheffield Green, Tomah Ivory.

Source:
1949-51 Mercury Passenger Car Prices and Options
1949-51 Mercury Passenger Car Data Books
1944-52 Mercury Body Parts Catalog

The beginning of the end. One of the first of the beautiful new '51 Mercury station wagons is pictured at the Ford test track in Dearborn in late 1950. But handcrafted beauty, alone, wouldn't save the custom wood-panelled wagons. Wood was out. Buyers wanted less upkeep, and that meant the future was in the all-steel station wagon.

IONIA WOOD

A footnote to the '49-51 Ford woodie story is the Ionia-Mitchell Co., of Ionia, Michigan. It was a wood station wagon body-builder for GM and Chrysler and built '60s Corvettes and concept cars. While it played a role, this firm did not build any of the '51 Ford station wagon bodies. Iron Mountain body plant manager Mark Swanson's tally sheets show production running to Dec. 5, 1951 — the day the assembly lines shutdown forever. At that time, the new '52 wagon models were in production at the Rouge. Where Ionia entered the picture was to supply wagon wood "replacement panels" for the Ford parts department. However, some Ionia wood panels, which were lighter-gauge and made different, did find their way onto Ford wagons at Iron Mountain. This may be explained by Ford having Ionia build a reserve of the special panels to offset some labor problems in 1951.

The last bodies of the "Famous Ford Woodies" were built at Iron Mountain December 5, 1951. One of the last – a '51 Country Squire model – is pictured at the famed Rouge manufacturing and assembly plant in Dearborn where the new generation of steel-bodied wagons would be produced. ◆

THE BODY NUMBERS
a sequential history

Serious collectors have always placed a higher value on anything with a maker's mark or serial number, from Roycroft pottery to Winchester rifles. It's what makes the thing more authentic and gives it more provenance and pedigree. It helps experts foil the fakers.

And so it is with the great works of American art, that most of the "woodies" built by or for Ford from 1928 to 1951, have body numbers. Though, like most other products made in series, the numerals weren't meant to please collectors or check against bogus copies, but were simply a maker's way to control quality and production.

The Ford station wagon numbers are in sequence from the first body built in a model series, to the last. Most can be found on a body tag attached to the engine compartment firewall, or — beginning with the 1940 models — hand-stamped into the firewall with large numerals. The numbering was done as the bodies came down the production line. They have no relationship to the car identification numbers stamped onto the chassis later at an assembly plant.

The bodies, built by The Murray Corporation of Detroit, or at Iron Mountain, Michigan, were handmade productions that required careful inspection to eliminate defects. By numbering them, it was a good way to backtrack problems down the line.

A 1940 *Ford News* article about Iron Mountain operations helps explain how this worked: "At the end of the final trim line, about one of every ten bodies is inspected in a fitting device set to the precise dimensions demanded in the finished product, and checked for accuracy. Variations of a fraction of an inch sends the unit back to the assembly line and this results in a checkup from the assembly starting point to determine where the error occurred."

In a 1952 interview, Iron Mountain body plant manager Mark Swanson explained how important it was to number the bodies while building the 1949-51 series. "I kept a record of the jobs okayed off the trim line each day," he said, "and a record of the rejected jobs, probably due to paint. If it was a paint sag or a run stain or a mar on the body, I had a record. I could trace it right back to the individual if it happened too often. That paid off. I could usually put my finger on things before they got out of control."

Swanson's Iron Mountain production reports, given to Ford woodie collector Cliff Helling of Minnesota some years ago are the basis for this chapter — which is the first attempt to set down each model year's numbering sequence. Written in the neat handwriting of one of his secretaries. Swanson gave a report of the precise number of station wagon bodies built each year at Iron Mountain from the late summer of '39 when production of the 1940 model began there — to the last one in 1951.

While no record of the true body numbers have been found, by knowing the first and last numbers in a wagon model sequence, production starting and ending dates, monthly plant capacity, and comparing with assembly plant production records, the likely body numbers stamped in a given month can be ascertained.

For the 1949-51 station wagons, Swanson's record provides the precise count of bodies built each month. It was easy to apply these to the running body numbers. At the end of the report is a note, probably in Swanson's hand: *"Total assembled bodies 1939 through December 5th, 1951 — 187,385."*

Why care about the numbers? It's just another thing that makes each one of those masterpiece Ford and Mercury woodies so "one-of-a-kind" special! "Ford woodies aren't just collector cars. They're numbered collector cars!" ◆

A 1940 Ford body, ready to be numbered on the firewall.

All but the mid-1930 to 1932 Ford woodies were numbered. An enlargement of the Iron Mountain photo from page 107 shows chalk location marks on the firewall for hammer-stamping a body number, which in 1940 was covered by the voltage regulator. The 1933-39 numbers were on a Murray Body tag attached to the firewall. The sequential numbers were for quality control. They now help collectors establish production history and authenticity.

The 1929-51 Ford woodies are American classics! Their sequential body numbers give them unique collector provenance and help establish dates they were built.

BODY BY MURRAY, 1929-39

1929-30 MODEL 150-A BODY NUMBERS

1929 assembly

1928

OCT-DEC	1 - 5	**1930 assembly**
1929		
JAN	6 - 600	5182 - 5346
FEB	601 - 1200	5347 - 5626
MAR	1201 - 1800	5627 - 6190
APRIL	1801 - 2400	6191 - 6430
MAY	2401 - 3000	6431 - **6529**
JUNE	3001 - 3600	
JULY	3601 - 4200	
AUG	4201 - 4500	
SEPT	4501 - 4675	
OCT	4676 - 4985	
NOV	4986 - 5181	

The 1929-30 model 150-A body station wagon numbers are on a Murray tag under the front seat. This sequence is based on Ford purchasing records of bodies delivered to assembly plants.

(NOTE. The 1930-31 model "150-B" and 1932 Ford station wagon bodies were not numbered)

The 1933-39 station wagon body numbers are to the right of the model type (860 in the example) on a Murray tag as shown attached to the engine firewall (unless removed). No records of these numbers exist. The ones here are matched to assembly records.

1933-34 FORD BODY NUMBERS

	1933 model	1934 model
JAN		1 - 158
FEB		159 - 463
MAR	1 - 3	464 - 793
APRIL	4 - 165	794 - 1123
MAY	166 - 405	1124 - 1453
JUNE	406 - 645	1454 - 1783
JULY	646 - 885	1784 - 2113
AUG	886 - 1125	2114 - 2443
SEPT	1126 - 1365	2444 - 2773
OCT	1366 - 1605	2774 - **3000**
NOV	1606 - 1845	
DEC	1846 - **2013**	

1935-39 FORD BODY NUMBERS
(approximate, based on production figures)

	1935 model	1936 model	*1937 model
SEPT		1-3 ('35 assy)	
OCT		4 - 281	('36 assy)
NOV		282 - 501	1 - 22
DEC		502 - 723	23- 350
1935 (assembly)		**1936**	**1937**
JAN	1- 315	724 - 1398	351 - 1378
FEB	316 - 815	1399 - 2073	1379 - 2428
MAR	816 - 1315	2074 - 2748	2429 - 3478
APRIL	1316 - 1865	2749 - 3423	3479 - 4528
MAY	1866 - 2315	3424 - 4098	4529 - 5578
JUNE	2316 - 2865	4099 - 4773	5579 - 6628
JULY	2866 - 3315	4774 - 5448	6629 - 7678
AUG	3316 - 3865	5449 - 6123	7679 - 8728
SEPT	3866 - 4315	6124 - 6798	8729 - 9150
OCT	4316 - **4536**	6799 - 6937	9151 - 9229
NOV		6938 - 7029	9230 - 9274
DEC		7030 - **7044**	9275 - **9304**

*Most 1937 station wagon body numbers are preceded by the Deluxe model "79B" (see page 80). Standard models are preceded by "790."

	1938 model	1939 model
		(combined Std/Dlx)
('37 assembly)		
DEC	1 - 911	
1938		
JAN	912 - 1761	1 - 668
FEB	1762 - 2611	669 - 1868
MARCH	2612 - 3461	1869 - 3068
APRIL	3462 - 4311	3069 - 4269
MAY	4312 - 5161	4270 - 5470
JUNE	5162 - 6011	5471 - 6670
JULY	6012 - 6426	6671 - 7861
AUG	6427 - 6816	7862 - **8266**
SEPT	6817 - **6944**	

BODY BY IRON MOUNTAIN, 1940-51

1940-42 FORD-MERCURY BODY NUMBERS

	1940 Ford (combined Std/Dlx)	1941 Ford-Merc (same body) ('40 assembly)	1942 Ford-Merc (same body) ('41 assembly)
('39 assembly)			
AUG-SEPT	1 - 575		1 - 179
OCT	576 - 1376	1 - 260	180 - 2120
NOV	1377 - 2177	261 - 761	2121 - 3702
DEC	2178 - 2876	762 - 1262	3703 - 4922
1940		**1941**	**1942**
JAN	2877 - 4376	1263 - 2697	4923 - 5855
FEB	4377 - 5876	2698 - 5134	5856 - **6833**
MAR	5877 - 7376	5135 - 7571	
APRIL	7377 - 8876	7572 - 10008	
MAY	8877 - 10376	10009 - 12445	
JUNE	10377 - 11224	12446 - 14882	
JULY	11225 - **11725**	14883 - 17319	
AUG		17320 - **19756**	

"Care of the wood paneling on the Station Wagon should be thought of in terms of boating rather than motoring. That is, the beauty and luster of the wood is protected by periodic varnishing instead of by waxing or polishing."

PREVENTIVE MAINTENANCE

Just as a yachtsman gives his craft a thorough revarnishing every season, so should you as a Station Wagon owner institute a program of periodic renewal of the finish. The wood paneling on your new Ford Station Wagon is similar in many respects to the planking on a yacht, but the conditions under which the finish must stand up are far more severe because of flying gravel, slush, road salt, and extremes of heat and cold.

CARE OF WOOD SURFACES

Under ordinary conditions of driving, a good varnish job should last a year or more. For ensuring complete protection, however, varnishing every Spring and Fall is recommended. Your Ford Dealer can readily handle the refinishing for you. If you want to do it yourself, here's how:

1: Clean wood finish of all dirt and wax. Remove tar spots, etc.

2: Lightly scuff surface with a fine grade of sandpaper. This provides a better bond between the old and new varnish coats. If any joints have loosened, seal with sealing compound. "Feather" edges of any cracks or blisters.

3: Spray on varnish coat, using a clear spar varnish of best quality, preferably Ford Spar Varnish. Work should be done in a place as dust-free as possible. If extra coats are needed, each one should be sanded before applying the next.

CARE OF STEEL SURFACES

The steel parts of the Station Wagon body have a baked enamel finish of exceptional beauty and long life. It should always be washed, rather than wiped or dusted. Dust particles on the surface act in much the same way as sandpaper when wiped with a cloth, causing minute scratches in the surface. This in turn tends to dull the finish and break it down. Occasional use of Ford Cleaner-Wax Polish will restore the original luster.

Most Important of All—

The most important thing of all in proper Station Wagon body care is also the easiest—regular and frequent washing. Keep it free of dirt, road salt and "traffic grime." Use plenty of clean, cold water—water is good for varnish, making it hard and bright. Never use wax on the wood panels. Your efforts will be well repaid in the continuing pleasure of driving a smart, shining car.

Finally, for long finish life your Station Wagon should be kept in a garage. Constant exposure to dew and strong sunlight has a harmful effect on any finish, even the extra-fine finish of your Ford.

HOW TO KEEP THAT *"Show-Room Complexion"*